An Introduction to Shakespeare's Late Plays

e₁

Also by Joe Nutt

John Donne: The Poems*
Breaking Eggs

*Also published by Palgrave

An Introduction to Shakespeare's Late Plays

JOE NUTT

palgrave

First published 2002 by
PALGRAVE
Houndmills, Basingstoke, Hampshire RG21 6XS and
175 Fifth Avenue, New York, N.Y. 10010
Companies and representatives throughout the world

PALGRAVE is the new global academic imprint of St. Martin's Press LLC Scholarly and Reference Division and Palgrave Publishers Ltd (formerly Macmillan Press Ltd).

ISBN 0–333–91462–7 hardcover
ISBN 0–333–91463–5 paperback

This book is printed on paper suitable for recycling and made from fully managed and sustained forest sources.

Cataloguing-in-publication data

A catalogue record for this book is available from the British Library.

A catalogue record for this book is available from the Library of Congress.

10 9 8 7 6 5 4 3 2 1
11 10 09 08 07 06 05 04 03 02

Printed in China

Contents

Preface

Most students embarking on a study of the late plays will not be newcomers to Shakespeare. It is highly likely that they will come to them after having studied some of his more famous works so it is important that students approach them aware of the degraded genre, romance, in which they find their roots. Critical stances entirely appropriate to the great tragedies come awry if applied to the late plays, which has partly accounted for their very mixed history in performance. It took a long time for scholars to correctly date them, and even longer to come to terms with the considerable gulf between their poetic and dramatic success.

In *Pericles*, for example, we find little in the way of credible characterisation at all, never mind the beautifully coherent and complex characterisation that permeates so much of Shakespeare's earlier work. Yet in *Cymbeline* and *The Winter's Tale* there are flashes of dialogue that render their speakers spectacularly unique and in the case of Leontes, every bit as psychologically convincing as the protagonists of the great tragedies.

Preconceptions are dangerous critical tools to use when handling the unfamiliar, and romance as a genre has become so debased that many students will realise they have no background knowledge of it at all. Shakespeare's use of romance sources has a controlling and crucial influence on romances as stage plays, and it frequently accounts for otherwise awkward dramatic features. It is the norm to find oneself swept into the midst of some powerful human tragedy or confrontation, with little warning and even less poetry. In the late plays Shakespeare appears consciously to focus on the purely dramatic situation in a much more immediate and urgent manner, as though the route to that wonderful moment has been wholly superseded by the moment itself.

However, in spite of the sketchy, hasty nature of many aspects of these plays, Shakespeare still employs his consummate grasp of poetic technique to articulate moments of deep emotion or poignancy, as in

Pericles' funeral words over Thaisa, or Imogen's parting from Post-humus. At such times it is common to find sharp contrasts in the verse symptomatic of the tension between source and script.

All four plays find their heart in the misery of family disruption and suffering, the source of their dramatic energy. In *Pericles*, a newly born family is apparently destroyed by fate at its very inception; in *Cymbeline*, a loving husband and wife are parted and a loving daughter is brought into implacable conflict with her father through deceit and treachery; in *The Winter's Tale*, sexual jealousy infects Leontes to such a degree that he publicly destroys his own family; and in *The Tempest*, filial rivalry, greed and ambition place a father and daughter at the mercy of the stormy elements. Each play shows us a family broken up by some implacable force, whether natural or human, but in all cases hope is never quite extinguished, and the promise of some kind of future glimmers through the misery and despair.

In all the plays we see how new identities, rather than merely being a comic device to create confusion, can be a means to avoid danger or bring about good. Disguise *per se* is of course a very familiar dramatic device, but in the late plays it is not only very common, but permeated by complex issues of deceit and corruption, rescue and safety.

Finally, in all four plays we encounter people enduring shocking extremes of suffering, wrong and ill fortune yet responding with courage, patience, fidelity, determination and constancy. Possibly the most distinguishing feature of the late plays is that they appear determined to exhibit humanity at its most admirable.

For Lucy

1

The Context of the Late Plays

A glance at any list of Shakespeare's plays covering the period of his theatrical career from 1589 to 1612, will show the four plays in this study, *Pericles*, *Cymbeline*, *The Winter's Tale* and *The Tempest*, huddled together at the end, perhaps with *Henry VIII* added on as the very last play. Since critical argument about precise dates of composition and performance has provided fertile ground for scholars for centuries, we can now, with some degree of confidence, agree they were written and performed between 1608 and 1612. A reasonable consensus would come up with this more precise list for the dates of composition:

1609 *Pericles*
1609 *Cymbeline*
1610 *The Winter's Tale*
1611 *The Tempest*
1612 *Henry VIII*

Dating Shakespeare's plays is a complex, usually imprecise business which can include an impressive variety of tools, from references to current events within the plays, to the more obvious evidence in external records such as the *Stationers' Register*, a public record of plays licensed for performance. But placing the plays in context means something much more than merely finding a date for them. What we need to do is gain some knowledge and understanding of how they fit into the wider historical period and culture of the day, and into the Shakespeare canon as a whole. This chapter attempts to provide both in a very basic way (readers who wish to develop their knowledge further will find useful books in the list of Further Reading).

The Elizabethan and Jacobean periods which Shakespeare's plays span were troubled and dangerous. The twin kernel of this potential instability and uncertainty lay in religion and in the monarchy. The event which, for the English, epitomises this, is the Gunpowder Plot of 1605, an event branded into cultural memories every November 5th to this day through the burning of Guy Fawkes in effigy on bonfires across the nation.

Once Henry VIII had elected to abandon the Catholic Church in 1534 via the Act of Supremacy, England found itself embroiled in religious conflict between Catholic and Protestant ideologies. There was nothing especially unusual in this; much of Europe was undergoing similar struggles as the omnipotence of the Pope in Rome was threatened doctrinally by reformers like John Calvin and Martin Luther, and politically by men like Henry. In England much of this controversy settled itself on the shoulders of the monarch, and both Elizabeth I and James I had to work hard to maintain their authority and command respect, amongst ambitious nobles and an underlying mistrust between Catholic and Protestant, whatever their social rank.

Shakespeare was born in 1564. By then Elizabeth, aged thirty-one, had been on the throne for six years. By the time he began writing plays in the early 1590s, she had maintained a strong hold on the nation for more than three decades. Life expectancy being what it was then, this was a considerable achievement and one characterised in the popular mind by peace and stability. Yet paradoxically, the violence and the cruelty of the state were terrifyingly extreme. Catholics were forbidden by law to practise their faith, priests were hunted down and executed, and Catholic families frequently fled London at night into the surrounding countryside under the shadow of rumours about Protestant attacks. The Catholic Mary Queen of Scots presented a constant threat to Elizabeth's rule until her trial and death in 1587. Anyone unfortunate enough to be caught conspiring against Elizabeth by the numerous spies run by her chief adviser, Robert

Cecil, faced appalling torture and a public death consciously designed to terrorise. James was equally savage in his handling of conspiracy, and the suffering inflicted on Guy Fawkes and his friends is not a research topic for the queasy.

We should also appreciate that the grim realities of disease and poor medical knowledge often combined to make the death of intimates or family members a familiar experience. Shakespeare's son Hamnet died aged eleven, leaving a surviving twin, Judith; and outbreaks of the plague in London killed thousands of otherwise healthy men, women and children. Some of the theatres doubled as bear pits or cock pits, and practices currently considered outrageously cruel were merely commonplace.

Another absolutely key aspect of Shakespeare's writing, which modern urban readers and students are wise to take into account, is his use of nature. He was a country boy, born in a town of only 1,500 inhabitants in the heart of the Warwickshire countryside, and this rural upbringing pulses through his poetry. Images of the natural world figure widely in his work and in ways that clearly indicate that he expects his audience to fully understand him. The London of the time was by today's standards a very small community, and the countryside was in easy reach. Hunting featured prominently in court life and huge areas were set aside for the Queen or King to hunt deer or wild boar with hounds, or employ falcons to kill smaller prey and wildfowl. A complex structure of etiquette and art surrounded the whole business of killing game, and images that exploit this common experience abound in Shakespeare. Similarly, we must understand that domestic conditions meant the individual's experience of the natural world was profoundly more intimate and meaningful than it is for most urban-bred students of today. Even the ordinary Londoner was tied to the physical conditions of climate and seasonal change in a way most people now would find difficult to grasp. This intimate familiarity is something Shakespeare expects from his audience, and he often consciously uses poetry to evoke the natural scene he is creating on stage. Today's audiences are used to all the tricks modern technology can employ to evoke physical settings, and so it is even more important, when we study Shakespeare, that we make an effort to understand his use of nature. A simple example would be his frequent references to kites, now an extremely rare bird of prey. Shakespeare's audiences would have known it as a common and repugnant scavenger, a vicious bird, often seen picking at the dead bodies of criminals and traitors left hanging on public display in the city.

Yet in this apparently ferocious state, English was finding its feet as a literary language, superseding Latin, and courtiers were as likely to exercise themselves with a pen as with a sword. The Renaissance fostered the expansion of the English language, and by the time it was over in around 1660 it had added over 10,000 new words to the language, from a whole range of foreign sources. Elizabeth's cleverly manipulative foreign policy, in which she skilfully used herself as nubile bait, meant that although England did take part in hostilities in France, the Netherlands and against Spain, these conflicts were short-lived and civil war seemed a thing of the past. She encouraged her nobles to play at military games rather than indulge in the real thing. When the Earl of Essex was actually in the field, he was a danger to her because as a man he exercised genuine military authority, while she often had to resort to mentioning her father, as a means to command similar respect. Some courtiers of the period complained of a lack of chivalric values and military skill, satirising the young men who took part in the *Accession Day Tilts*, a jousting pageant put on by Elizabeth in which one sought advancement not through the blood and horror of war, but by impressing the Queen, who was, after all, a woman. The ultimately successful courtiers like Burghley and Cecil were arch civil servants, not soldiers, and the power of the state rested not on the daring actions of its heroes, Ralegh, Drake or Essex, but on the cunning of its diplomats, who were all learned men. Elizabeth herself was extremely well educated and able to match any one of her advisers, and although it is difficult to speak of a true Renaissance in Elizabeth's England in the same way we might of Italy, her state was indeed one which valued art every bit as highly as it valued military might or commerce.

Not surprisingly in such circumstances, the theatre lived a vital but precarious existence itself, subject to official control and censorship whenever times became especially unstable and always under suspicion from those in authority because of its great power to debate.

Shakespeare wrote eleven plays with the word 'king' in the title, and if you add *Julius Caesar, Hamlet, Titus Andronicus, Macbeth, Coriolanus, Antony and Cleopatra, Pericles, Cymbeline* and *The Winter's Tale*, you find 20 plays out of 37 dealing with notions of the monarchy. Shakespeare's own theatre company changed its name from the Lord Chamberlain's Men to the King's Men, performing at court, after Elizabeth's death in 1603. An ambiguous shift, since it reflected not only the theatre's interest in the security of royal patronage but James's own insecurity.

This royal patronage did not mean, however, that the theatre was the least bit elitist. Quite the opposite was true. Elizabethan theatre was peculiar in one respect, that it captured the interest (and financial patronage) of every social rank, from the monarch to the youthful apprentices whose masters complained about their absenting themselves from work to attend the afternoon performances. Although some performances took place indoors at private, often royal venues, by far the widest experience of theatre was in the large outdoor playhouses like the Globe, now so painstakingly reconstructed on London's South Bank. Performances took place even during the winter, in the afternoons, although the combination of heat and plague in the summer often saw all the theatres closed by the city authorities. The theatre was enormously popular, the companies extremely busy, and by the time Shakespeare was retiring and passing on his role as chief playwright for the King's Men to John Fletcher, his company had become profitable enough to open a new indoor theatre at Blackfriars as well as running the Globe.

Yet, however central a part Shakespeare came to play in the culture of his age, we know virtually nothing of significance about the Englishman who bore his name. One of the characteristics which may well lay claim to account for his being considered a genius is that however hard we may search, it is impossible to find any view or opinion, in any one of his plays, which we can confidently assert to be his own. No other English dramatist vanishes so deftly behind the complexities of his work. It is possible to read his entire sonnet sequence and still feel absolutely ignorant of the individual human being who created it, something unimaginable with other poets and playwrights of the period. One unfortunate side effect of this anonymity is that strenuous scholarly efforts (and more worryingly, non-scholarly) are made to construct the most elaborate fantasies about him, on the flimsiest of foundations. The debate centring on the possibility that the Earl of Oxford, Edward De Vere, a man who died in 1604, wrote Shakespeare's plays, is just one more in a long list.

In effect, when we use the word 'Shakespeare' today, it is, in a unique way, quite significantly different from the way we might refer to Jonson or Marlowe. As Jonathan Bate demonstrates so well in his book *The Genius of Shakespeare* (Picador, 1997), centuries of performance, study and scholarly attention have turned the word 'Shakespeare' into something far more profound and complex than a playwright's name. It immediately connotes his entire body of work, the unique position he commands in world literature, and associated ideas of his supremacy as a poet and dramatist. Post-Freudian literary criticism has driven such deep inroads into our educational systems that it is almost an expectation from students that, somewhere in their studies, they will encounter information about a writer's life and how it informs his or her work. This is simply not possible with Shakespeare, although that has of course not prevented various attempts. A mild example is E. K. Chambers, who, in his book *Shakespeare: A Survey* (Penguin, 1964, pp. 216–17), argued that Shakespeare must have suffered some kind of breakdown between the writing of *Timon of Athens* and *Pericles*, which would account for the severe differences between the two plays. Which leads us on to how the late plays fit into the canon as a whole.

One of the most popular critical stances taken by scholars interested in the late plays is to seek some sense of finality in them. The mere fact that they come at the end of Shakespeare's career seems to encourage us to look for something which will neatly conclude both that career and Shakespeare's entire dramatic vision. Such attempts, however, are doomed from the start since they rely on accepting not only that Shakespeare saw himself as consciously constructing such a career, but that he was somehow uniquely immune to the theatrical trends and fashions around him.

We do know that if it were not for the efforts of two of his theatrical friends, John Heminges and Henry Condell, who after his death went to some trouble to produce the printed edition of his plays we now refer to as the First Folio, there might never have been a 'Shakespeare'. Not until Ben Jonson decided it was a good idea, did any playwright of the period consider having his plays printed in book form for others to read. Equally, the obvious interest in stage spectacle that sprinkles these plays (Imogen's discovery of Cloten's headless corpse, or Hermione's resurrection) shows that he was using dramatic elements wholly in keeping with the taste of his younger, Jacobean contemporaries.

Yet the late plays quite clearly form an identifiable group. They are often referred to as romances, a term which needs some explanation here since its modern connotations are many and various. To the Renaissance reader the romance was a form more familiar in verse or prose than drama. In fact many inherent features of romance as a genre make it extremely problematic to dramatise. It involved the sublime love relationships of kings and princes, heroism, exotic locations and swift and unpredictable changes in fortune frequently generated by divine will. Much of the action took place in either courtly settings or Arcadian ones, the heroes' changing fortunes leading them between the two, often to find love where it was least expected but ultimately most fitting. Although romances were widespread throughout Europe, in English Sir Philip Sidney's *Arcadia* and Edmund Spenser's *The Faerie Queene* were the two most well known romances of the age.

The bizarre complexities of the action, the intense scheming and manipulation that goes on, yet the perfect justice meted out in the wholly conventional happy ending, all contribute to the reader's sense of the romance as a highly artificial and perhaps slightly inferior form. Critics like Dryden write about 'ridiculous and incoherent' stories, 'grounded on impossibilities'. Ben Jonson termed *Pericles* 'a mouldy tale', and numerous poets and scholars in the two centuries immediately after Shakespeare's death felt unable to believe any of these four plays could really be by Shakespeare, their substance appeared to be so slight. Yet undoubtedly, as E. C. Petett argued in his *Shakespeare and the Romance Tradition* (Methuen, 1970), these plays clearly owe a great deal to this inferior genre.

They do include many of the romance features outlined above, but as they are also 'Shakespeare', there is a critical eagerness to find ways to redeem them from the accusation of lacking seriousness. One route out of this dilemma is to see them as experimental. In his edition of *Cymbeline* (the Arden Shakespeare, Methuen, 1984) J. M. Nosworthy argues this most cogently, viewing *Pericles* and *Cymbeline* as steps on the way to the far more successful *The Winter's Tale* and *The Tempest*. He also suggests that they are unromantically glossed with a tragic vision left over from writing the great tragedies. The court masque had become increasingly popular, a private theatrical event characterised as much by lavish show as dramatic content, and it is also argued that the late plays lean in this direction. That rich show formed part of Elizabeth's court is easily seen in any of her portraits, where extravagant jewellery, intricate lace or delicately embroidered silk feature prominently. James perhaps outdid her, and it was possible for a guest to attend a banquet in his honour at which the astonishing wealth of exotic food on view was whisked away before a morsel of it passed anyone's lips, and a far more lavish feast replaced it. What, then, can we draw from these rich contests?

Amidst the various possibilities, what we can accept as significant starting points are: that the late plays display sufficient common features to make it entirely sensible to treat them and study them as a group; that they mark a departure from Shakespeare's work up until that date; that they show signs of being influenced by theatrical trends of the period; and that they seek to generate an audience response strikingly different from all his other plays.

The historical and cultural context takes on even greater significance today since it has become accepted academic practice to build the study of Shakespeare's plays into courses with overtly different agendas. It is now difficult to engage with the plays untrammelled by a given political or social framework within which the work must take place. No such intention informs this study. Throughout, the emphasis falls on how to engage imaginatively with the text for what it is, a script from which professional theatrical practitioners create drama.

In each case the discussion that follows looks at the main features of the play in terms of both theme and language. Key elements here are the ideas of family disruption at the start of the plays and the harmony of their endings, but also significant are the ideas of identity, magic and suffering.

Each chapter deals with a single play under eight headings that emphasise how closely linked the four plays are, helping the reader to explore the purely human concerns which lie at the very core of the late plays.

2

Pericles

Estrangement and Family Disruption

One of the most compelling dramatic features of the late plays is the way in which they bring to life potent relationships within family units, frequently capturing our early interest through moving scenes of separation and loss. A characteristic scene is Act 3, Scene i, of *Pericles*, which will also serve to draw attention to a number of other features of the romances.

In *Pericles*, Act 3, Scene i, having earned the hatred of an incestuous king; fled his own city, Tyre, to escape murder; been shipwrecked; wooed, won and married a princess, Pericles finds himself once more buffeted by the gods as he is returning triumphantly back to Tyre with his pregnant wife.

Whatever else its shortcomings, no one can condemn *Pericles* as dull. At this point in the near ceaseless action, Lychorida enters the stage carrying a child, Marina (Pericles has just been seen pleading with the gods to calm the terrifying storm and aid his wife who is giving birth). Yet Lychorida's opening words jar horribly with our expectations of joy at the birth of a first child, and instead are full of foreboding and fear. The child would die if it had sense, she suggests, as she would do herself, and then Shakespeare gives us just enough time to consider the import of this strange wish, before Lychorida adds, 'Take in your arms this piece / Of your dead queen' (3.i.17–18).

The dramatic shock is intense. It is as much news to the audience as it is to Pericles, which allows us to empathise closely when he roars his distress, as he must do if we are to make sense of Lychorida's subsequent injunction, 'do not assist the storm' (l. 19). The rest of Lychorida's speech is remarkably simple and direct. She addresses the heart of the situation without frills or gloss of any kind. She offers the baby to Pericles and reminds him that it is part of his wife, indeed the only part left alive, and now it relies utterly upon him for its own life and safety. One of the things we will repeatedly encounter in these plays is precisely this directness and simplicity. It is present, too, in Pericles' response.

This ought to surprise us somewhat if we are familiar with the tragedies, where characters under at least as much pressure as Pericles is here, produce powerful and memorable images to explore their dilemma. 'As flies to wanton boys are we to the gods,' says Gloucester in *King Lear*, 'They kill us for their sport' (4.i.36–7). 'Out, out brief candle,' says Macbeth, 'Life's but a walking shadow' (*Macbeth*, 5.v.23–4); both speeches challenge us to think about larger issues and meanings. Pericles is stunningly less articulate and can only manage,

> O you gods!
> Why do you make us love your goodly gifts,
> And snatch them straight away?
>
> (3.i.22–4)

Lychorida, witnessing Pericles' weak complaint, replies in equally simple terms, 'Patience, good sir,' which may seem mere repetition, as she has used precisely the same phrase in line 19. But patience is a key concept in the late plays and Shakespeare appears not to be above repeating it to make that quite clear.

Pericles' next speech, however, raises the poetic tone.

> Now, mild may be thy life!
> For a more blusterous birth had never babe;
> Quiet and gentle thy conditions! For
> Thou art the rudliest welcome to this world
> That e'er was prince's child. Happy what follows!

Thou hast had as chiding a nativity
As fire, air, water, earth and heaven can make,
To herald thee from the womb. [Poor inch of nature!]
Even at the first thy loss is more than can
Thy portage quit, with all thou canst find here.
Now the good gods throw their best eyes upon't!

(3.i.27–37)

The opening lines are balanced around the use of 'for' and the rhythm is unhurried, formal, even contemplative. Pericles has the presence of mind not only to employ a list, 'As fire, air, water, earth' (l. 33), but by adding 'heaven' to it, he cleverly leads into a concluding prayer, 'Now the good gods throw their best eyes upon't!' (l. 37). There is also the parenthetic 'Poor inch of nature' (l. 34), which comes after the heaviest caesura imaginable and might be used to accompany the profound gaze of recognition entirely natural between father and new-born child. Pericles is holding his first child in his arms amidst a terrible, life-threatening storm, while his wife lies dead below decks, yet *all* his concern here is for the child's future. Even when reminding himself of her dead mother, 'Even at the first thy loss is more than can / Thy portage quit' (ll. 35–6), his thoughts return immediately to his child and her future.

What can we make of this apparently contradictory response where, within a few stage moments, Pericles is seen accusing the gods of being extraordinarily inimical to himself, and then pleading for them to watch over his daughter? If we are seeking the kind of complicated yet consistent psychological reasoning we have come to expect in a Shakespearean tragic hero, where the most subtle workings of his mind are presented to us via a soliloquy, in *Pericles* we are going to be frequently frustrated. Instead what we have here is material heavily dependent on another type of source entirely. A dead queen, the birth of a princess, a wise nurse, this is the stuff of folk and fairy tale. What Pericles is doing in wishing a happy life for his child is entirely conventional in fairy tale terms. The late plays, via their romance sources, owe a great deal to folk and fairy tale and it is prudent to remember this as we look at the way Shakespeare handles scenes such as this.

The sailors now remind us of the danger all are in, and Shakespeare takes care to make their conventional prose fit the exigent dramatic situation. Their words are full of stormy description, importunity and fear, 'the brine and cloudy billow kiss the moon', 'your queen must overboard', 'briefly yield 'er, for she must overboard straight'. That Pericles succumbs so readily and easily to their superstitious wishes might also give us pause for thought, yet if we note he uses the formal 'queen' to refer to his wife, we can again see that it is the fairy-tale thrust of plot which Shakespeare is exploring rather than any psychological realism or complex characterisation. One of the troublesome features of the late plays is this type of dramatic energy, where the need to flag the potential future for the audience takes precedence over the finer characterisation which we might have become used to studying Shakespeare's earlier plays.

That the dramatic experience of this play is fundamentally different from earlier Shakespeare is something we might glean from a brief look at its sources.

Shakespeare was a remarkably skilful adapter of varied sources, whether historical, like Holinshed's *Chronicles*, or romances, like John Gower's *Confessio Amantis*, the chief source for *Pericles*. Gower's poem was written sometime towards the end of the fourteenth century but there are printed versions of it dated 1532 and 1534, and the story it tells of Prince Apollonius of Tyre is, as Ben Jonson famously described it, a thoroughly 'mouldy tale', one told and retold, orally and in literature, for centuries. In these romance tales the heroes travel erratically, endure pendulously sweeping changes of fortune but are usually rewarded for their patience. Lengthy passages of time play a central role in them, and it is therefore inevitable that in adapting them for the Jacobean stage, Shakespeare found himself pressed to employ techniques that could allow for this. If we think of how soon Viola becomes Orsino's favourite, Caesario, in *Twelfth Night*, or how long it takes Hamlet to carry out his revenge, real time is something Shakespeare treats rather cavalierly in earlier plays, since it was dramatic time which most concerned him. But the importance placed on the passage of real time in romances, the span of someone's life, impinges heavily on Shakespeare's control of stage time. What matters is that Pericles is deprived of his wife almost as soon as he has found her, which is why Shakespeare takes us straight from Pentapolis to Thaisa's death bed via a simple dumb show and Gower's chorus at the start of Act 3.

If we look at Lychorida's words over her dead mistress, 'Here she lies, sir' (3.i.54), and we are alert to thinking in terms of using the poetry to help us imagine the theatrical event, we should recognise a very simple dramatic problem. No change of scene has been indicated, yet clearly Thaisa's death occurred off stage as Lychorida had to enter to answer Pericles' call (l. 14). How, then, can the two actors playing Pericles and Thaisa be conveyed to that same place in the space of Lychorida's four words? Almost certainly a curtain at the rear of the stage would have been drawn to reveal Thaisa's body and to convey the idea of below decks, which is neat, efficient and time-saving. The effect is to focus attention on Pericles' elegy over the dead Thaisa (ll. 56–69), in itself a fascinating example of why the late plays can prove so problematic theatrically.

The speech is clearly divided into two at line 64 where Pericles ceases his mourning and then issues instructions to Lychorida. The first half, one lengthy, complex sentence, is entirely what we might expect from almost any mature Shakespearean verse. Pericles stresses the stark, cruel conditions of Thaisa's confinement without even the comfort of light or fire, and the weight of the rhythm falls heavily on the phrase, 'Forgot thee utterly'; he then bemoans the circumstance that means Thaisa is even to be denied the dignity of a decent burial. There is lyrical poignancy in the image of Thaisa cast, 'scarcely coffin'd, in the ooze', before the inhumanity of what is happening is stressed further through the idea that instead of lights and funeral songs, only 'the belching whale' and 'humming water' will act as her monuments. We may also respond deeply to the reference to our essential human frailty in the final image of her body 'Lying with simple shells'. There is a predominance of soft syllables, sounds like 's's and 'm's, that suit the mournful tone. It is a graceful, touching elegy, however brief, and one calculated to touch the audience's heart. But it is only half a speech.

In sharp contrast, the latter sentence (and second half of the speech) is all bustle and imperative practicality, and at first may appear wholly inappropriate. Pericles orders Lychorida to fetch a list of curious items and to place Marina safely 'Upon the pillow' while he says 'A priestly farewell' to his dead wife. Shakespeare is writing for an unquestioningly Christian audience for whom the ritual of the last rites was a vital matter, to be neglected at the peril of one's eternal soul. The idea of a secular figure performing the ceremony as well as they could, if circumstances meant it was impossible to find a priest, would have been entirely commonplace. Pericles' final, impatient 'Suddenly, woman' as he instructs Lychorida, also effectively, returns us to the frenzied action and danger of the storm, before the sailors reappear to re-establish that dramatic tone.

We might reasonably ask, why has Shakespeare chosen to divide the speech so distinctly in this way? In fact why include the latter half at all? Once again it is the pressure of the romance source that largely determines this. The source insists that Thaisa must be found alive and richly coffined with all the trappings of royalty that will one day be needed to prove her identity, and this information has to be conveyed, so Shakespeare does it as quickly and efficiently as possible, in part cloaking it with Pericles' elegiac grief. But it is also characteristic of these plays to combine rich lyrical passages with action in this way so that we are conscious of their 'romance' nature.

Flight and Foreigners

A significant number of the central figures in these plays choose to flee their home in the face of mortal danger or familial disruption. Their departures are usually abrupt, dramatic, and take them to places with exotic names like Pentapolis or Bohemia that Shakespeare's audience would know only as foreign, although the unfortunate Imogen in *Cymbeline*, strays only as far as the wilds of Wales.

In Act 1, Scene ii, Pericles is confronted by one of his most loyal noblemen, Helicanus, because Pericles' introversion and lassitude since his return from Antioch has caused his courtiers great anxiety. Appreciating that Helicanus's concern is for both him and the state, Pericles decides to unburden himself.

The first thing that should strike us is how lacking in action this entire scene is. We have two characters together on stage, in private conversation, and nothing disturbs or interrupts the flow of their dialogue at all. The bulk of the dialogue belongs to Pericles, who in some 33 lines, recounts what has taken place in Antioch before using it to explain his curious behaviour. At line 94, the flow of his speech is interrupted by Helicanus's 'Alas, sir!' which completes the line of verse. What are we to make of this dramatically intransigent material?

A closer consideration of the tone and structure of this unwieldy scene brings some surprising results. Pericles starts by signalling the need to listen carefully. Shakespeare is perfectly aware of the dramatic dangers, and requests his audience's attention by dramatising Helicanus as an attentive listener. 'Attend me then' (l. 70), Pericles says, and whatever physical action we might choose for the actor playing Helicanus here, it must suggest he does what his king asks. That is, of course, a way of drawing the audience into a similar state of mind. Pericles explains how he visited Antioch with the express purpose of winning Antiochus's daughter as his bride, but he adds an element of regal responsibility to 'bring joys to' his subjects. At this point, though, the speech seems to exhibit signs of corruption.

The quarto edition of *Pericles* is a notoriously corrupt text for editors to work from and there are places where, for a whole range of reasons, editors are still unsure of the original intention. One of those occurs in line 74. The work of previous editors is of course available for us in whatever text we are using, but even the most assertive Shakespearean editor sometimes has to throw up his hands, and in the late plays there are proportionately more of these incidences than in earlier plays. We can expose the difficulty by the addition of bold type to indicate it precisely.

> I went to Antioch,
> Whereas thou know'st, against the face of death
> I sought the purchase of a glorious beauty,
> From whence an issue I might propagate,
> **Are arms to** princes and bring joys to subjects.
>
> (1.ii.70–4)

However corrupt the text here, we can find an underlying meaning which is both sensible and fitting. Pericles sought a wife, not merely selfishly, but in order to provide an heir for the state, and it is a rhetorical point he makes, that such children give strength not only to their parents, but also to the state and all its subjects, who rejoice in this.

Moving on, but maintaining an unclouded focus on the verse, in the gentle rhythm of line 75, 'Her face was to mine eye, beyond all wonder', we can hear something of Pericles' awe and sadness at his discovery of the ugly truth behind the princess's beautiful exterior, that she is her father's mistress and that the answer to the riddle is, 'as black as incest'. This prevalence of 's' sounds continues through lines 76 to 79 where the rhythm invites us to linger on 'smooth' (l. 78) before culminating in the clipped 'kiss'.

Pericles now begins to do something much more usual in a Shakespearean hero; he gives us his most intimate thoughts about Antioch. But amidst several lengthy, even quite complex sentences, we find a brief sentence made up of two lines, which also rhyme:

> I knew him tyrannous; and tyrants' fears
> Decrease not, but grow faster than the years.
>
> (1.ii.84–5)

How can we explain this sudden contrast? Shakespeare uses rhyming couplets throughout his work and especially in his earlier plays, where whole speeches can sometimes be in couplets. But a couplet which crops up abruptly like this, in the middle of otherwise undisturbed blank verse, requires some explanation. What Pericles is doing here is making a sententious observation about human experience drawn from this one particular example. His encounter with Antiochus has reminded him that all tyrants live in fear for their lives, and their reigns inevitably become increasingly insecure.

There is also something fashionably witty about the toying with the word 'doubt' which follows, as Pericles expresses his justifiable fear that Antiochus is himself afraid Pericles will make public his incest. This is closely followed by a second rhyming couplet.

> When **all**, for mine if I may call offence,
> **Must feel** war's blow, who spares not innocence.
>
> (1.ii.92–3)

Here again, we appear to have a *sententia*, though admittedly a rather weak one, which becomes clearer when we link the subject and the verb, as indicated with bold type, and realise that 'who' refers back to war. That war destroys both the guilty and the innocent alike may still seem something of a commonplace rather than a pearl of wisdom. But there is an alternative reason for this positioning of the couplet.

There remain only two lines before Helicanus interrupts, but if we examine closely the dramatic nature of the interruption we can formulate a much clearer vision of the stage event. Pericles' account of the threat to himself and Tyre now posed by Antiochus is a lengthy, fluent sentence, yet neither especially measured nor sedate. The rhythm suggests a degree of excitement or urgency that is entirely understandable if we remember that Pericles is unburdening himself. He has lived with the dark secret about Antiochus, in fear of his life, alone, and with the knowledge that 'many worthy princes' bloods were shed', for some time. Therefore it is something of a relief to tell someone else at last. We would expect such a revelation to be hurried and even impatient, and the verse indicates this most strongly where the rhyming couplet (ll. 92–3) would appear to end the speech, but Pericles finds an afterthought to tack onto it, and it is that afterthought which Helicanus interrupts. Remove Helicanus's words entirely, as below, and the structure of the speech immediately strikes us as dramatically coherent; and of course, it ends with a rhyming couplet, now at lines 99–100. Bold type again can make this clearer by linking the key subject and verb.

> Which **love** to all, of which thyself art one,
> Who now reprov'dst me for't, –
> **Drew** sleep out of mine eyes, blood from my cheeks,
> Musings into my mind, with thousand doubts
> How I might stop this tempest ere it came;
> And finding little comfort to relieve them,
> I thought it princely charity to grieve them.
>
> (1.ii.94–100)

What this entails on stage is the actor playing Pericles barely taking a breath to permit Helicanus to interrupt. In fact it is not really an interruption, but something modern actors would recognise as over-lapping.

To complete our analysis of the dramatic potential of this scene, we need only now note how direct, measured and clear Helicanus's response (ll. 101–10) is. A caesura, 'Freely will I speak. Antiochus you fear' (l. 102), indicates the precise point at which Helicanus begins his advice, which essentially consists of just four simple points – Antiochus is a threat to you; escape him by travelling until he gives up or dies; leave the state in the hands of someone you trust; if you choose me, I will prove absolutely trustworthy. Pericles' excitable anxiety contrasts markedly with this measured reason and Helicanus is established as the unshakeably loyal regent he proves to be.

The late plays have frequently been condemned as difficult, un-dramatic texts to perform, full of awkward episodes, lacking in psychological realism, marred by absurd coincidence. Certainly there are difficulties in scenes such as those discussed here, but once we see how the verse works and informs the action on stage, then they take on a new life.

New Identities

Disguise and the subsequent confusion it creates are highly conven-tional features of Shakespearean comedy. One comedy after another is seen to revolve around the muddle and amusement created when one person (or more) is mistaken for another. Although Shakespeare uses disguise with great success in tragedy too, for example Edgar in *King Lear*, it is otherwise noticeably missing from his tragic outlook. In the late plays, disguise, or in extreme cases the adoption of a wholly new identity, is a common occurrence but the ends it serves are quite different from those of Shakespearean comedy.

In *Pericles*, for example, Marina is saved from death at the hands of the murderer, Leonine, by marauding pirates, who then sell her, as a virgin, to the owner of a brothel in Mytilene. Boult, the servant of the brothel owner and his wife, is told to go out and search for a fresh, suitable girl since their current stable is not bringing in much of a profit: 'The stuff we have, a strong wind will blow it to pieces, they are so pitifully sodden' (4.ii.17–18). This is a peculiarly brash and distasteful image, even for Jacobean theatre. You would search hard to find anything as bitingly ugly even in Webster. It is important because it provides a backdrop to the discussion which eventually takes place between the Bawd and Marina.

The Pandar decides to buy her, exits with the Pirates to pay them, and tells his wife to prepare Marina: 'instruct her what she has to do, that she may not be raw in her entertainment' (ll. 50–1). The unprepossessing word 'raw' underscores the benefits of a very close analytical reading. In one sense we know it refers to Marina being innocent, a novice whore. The word 'green' might have been equally expected, but we have 'raw', not 'green'. The effect, taken in conjunction with earlier imagery used of the brothel inmates, is to sharpen our sense of Marina's danger and increase our sympathy. Something 'raw' is also something vulnerable, something acutely sensitive to touch and we wince at the Pandar's ugly sense of humour. It is Marina's vulnerability, her innocence and weakness which is at the heart of her conflict with the brothel's inhabitants, something which takes on even greater significance when we come to consider what happens to Perdita, Miranda and Imogen in the other romances.

The Bawd then accentuates this by telling Boult to advertise not just Marina's physical beauty but particularly her virginity, since 'Such a maidenhead were no cheap thing if men were as they have been' (ll. 55–6). Knowing her virginity now to be the object of an auction, Marina gives her first response:

> Alack that Leonine was so slack, so slow!
> He should have struck, not spoke; or that these pirates
> Not enough barbarous, had not o'erboard
> Thrown me for to seek my mother!
>
> (4.ii.60–3)

The Bawd's response, 'Why lament you, pretty one?' (l. 64), guides our interpretation of Marina's words. It is a 'lament', a pitifully sad song. The acute sensibility to sound, evinced by the first line and half, 'Alack that Leonine was so slack, so slow! / He should have struck, not spoke', where the harsh 'Alack', 'slack' and 'struck' clash jarringly with the gentle 'so', 'so slow' and 'spoke', is hardly accidental. Similarly, Marina's choice of death, being thrown overboard 'for to seek my mother', besides being poetically apt for her, is in the language of fairy tale and myth.

The exchange of views between Marina and the Bawd continues to reward close analysis. The endearment 'pretty one' the Bawd uses suggests she responds gently to Marina's pitiful wish for death, and also draws on the language of fairy tale. Marina's terse reply, 'That I am pretty' (l. 65), is both direct and challenging. What other young heroine in Shakespeare ever regrets her beauty? The Bawd appears to maintain her sympathetic tone in her comforting suggestion that Marina owes her looks to the gods and she should therefore consider herself fortunate, but Marina, in contrast to her father on board the ship of her birth, remains stolidly stoical, yet expresses herself in the simplest manner possible, 'I accuse them not' (l. 67). Beneath her simplicity there is, however, another challenge and the implication that she does accuse others, a hint the Bawd doesn't yet take. Instead she retries the idea that it is fortune which has brought Marina here, with the added reminder that this, at least, means she continues to live. Marina's lament, we recall, concentrated on her wish to die. Her extreme virtue begins to show itself now when she is prepared to accuse herself for failing to die at Leonine's hands. The Bawd's response, 'Ay, and you shall live in pleasure' (l. 72), then gives us a strong clue to the pace of this exchange. Her opening 'Ay' links it firmly to her previous speech, and this is made even clearer by the use of the same main verb 'live'. Marina's intervening speech, therefore, has to be delivered at some speed if the Bawd's insistent tone is to work. An actress playing Marina, speaking reflectively of her 'fault', would make it impossible for the Bawd's two speeches to connect in the way their content suggests. The Bawd's new temptation, 'you shall live in pleasure', is ironically ill-suited for this particular girl and the idea that speed is the essence of this exchange becomes even clearer as Marina resorts to the most direct denial possible, 'No' (l. 73), and nothing else. The exchange now risks turning into a clumsy, even childish argument as the Bawd instantly replies with 'Yes, indeed you shall', but she keeps a cooler head for the moment, and having failed with fortune and pleasure, she tries wealth and status, 'and taste gentlemen of all fashions. You shall fare well; you shall have the difference of all complexions' (ll. 74–6). The childish shift in the argument becomes most obvious now as Marina simply stops her ears to the Bawd's glib temptations and brings this rapid burst of dialogue to its first major pause.

It is difficult to envisage Marina's assertive question, 'Are you a woman?' being delivered at the same fast pace, because it is so clearly both a minor victory and a question which requires some thought. The Bawd is indeed baffled by it and answers confusedly, 'What would you have me be and I be not a woman?' (4.ii.78–9), implying that of course she's a woman – what else could she be? That allows Marina to make her point and the word 'honest' successfully carries the moral authority Marina wishes it to, since the Bawd is finally moved to anger. So far she has been sympathetic, at least superficially, but Marina has charged her with corruption, a crime she knows only too well she is inescapably guilty of, and so the pretence is no longer worth keeping up. From this point it is evident that the Bawd's tone has changed. The oaths and threats, 'Marry, whip thee, gosling', 'Come, you're a young foolish sapling, and must be bow'd as I would have you' (ll. 82–4), imply some undetermined physical action between the Bawd and Marina, as does Marina's plea, 'The gods defend me!' (l. 86). There is no further argument or discussion. The child is being reprimanded but the corruption of the maternal figure, the Bawd, is emphasised in her final crude images, 'men must comfort you, men must feed you, men stir you up' (ll. 88–9). Only Boult's return seems to save Marina from further punishment and humiliation.

The innocent victim of Dionyza's jealousy, Marina has, like her father, been forced to live amongst strangers, in a new land. She places her trust in the gods, but the human forces that control her are free to eradicate her identity and give her a new one. What Boult advertises around Mytilene is a new virgin for sale in his master's brothel; Marina, the daughter of King Pericles of Tyre, is dead to the wider world. As we will see later, this is a recurrent pattern in the romances; characters lose their old identities for new, becoming different in return. It is why the romances seem to offer some larger message about the cycle of life.

Trials and Tests

Many characters in the late plays are made to endure tests or trials of some kind. Hermione is formally arraigned for adultery before Leontes' court in *The Winter's Tale*, and the entire last scene of *Cymbeline* consists of a kind of impromptu court in which every imaginable score in the play is settled, and some remarkably flappy ends are firmly knotted. But more often the tests individuals face are informal and very private. Pericles has to solve a riddle to win Antiochus's daughter, Ferdinand has to carry logs from A to B to appease Prospero, and Marina has to preserve her virginity in, of all places, a brothel.

Marina's trial presents a severe challenge to theatrical practitioners. Against the overtly corrupt and ugly background of the brothel, which is strongly evoked by the language used by the Pandar, the Bawd and Boult, however we might choose to physically represent it on stage, Marina's virtue has to shine so brightly that in a short space of time she can completely neutralise Lysimachus's lust. Realism could be a problem here. We might find a way out of this dilemma by invoking the idea of fairy tale, but that is not so easy in this case. Unlike, for example, Ferdinand's having to work to pacify Prospero, Marina's defence of her virtue is not such a readily recognisable fairy-tale motif.

In terms of staging, we can usefully divide Marina's trial into three. The first section is Lysimachus's arrival and the pleasantries he exchanges with the corrupt inmates of the brothel (4.vi.19–46). The second consists of the Bawd's advice to Marina (ll. 47–64), and the last section is Marina's triumphant conversion of Lysimachus (ll. 65–120). Analysing each in turn provides a picture of how they function within themselves, but, more importantly, how they cohere.

Lysimachus's opening remark, 'How now! How a dozen of virginities?' (l. 19), is immediately problematic. We learn from the conversation between the brothel inmates that precedes his entrance that he is here in disguise, yet he speaks openly and with obvious familiarity. He jokes about the cost of virginity, debasing them and himself by referring to virginity as one might any domestic commodity. What is more, the Bawd immediately addresses him not only as she would a regular customer, but also as 'your honour' (l. 20), and Boult makes his failure of disguise even worse by adding, 'I am glad to see your honour in good health' (l. 21), an obviously knowing remark considering the fate of other brothel customers. This darkly familiar humour continues in Lysimachus's comment about the healthy legs of the brothel's customers, which is entirely in keeping with the ugly language of the others already noted. Marina's virginity becomes something far more powerful than the assumed virtue of fairy-tale maidens when juxtaposed in this way with the terminal reality of venereal disease. The effect is also enhanced by the conversation about Marina which has taken place before Lysimachus enters, in which there is a distinctly black comedy created by the idea that Marina has already turned away all potential purchasers and is, as the Bawd says, able to 'make a puritan of the devil' (l. 9). This is a dramatic contrast to our expectations since we last saw Marina firmly in the hands of the Bawd and Boult, who had no doubt that he would return that night with some of 'the lewdly inclin'd' (4.ii.142). It is vital that we know of Marina's success so far in preserving her virginity if we are to anticipate the coming encounter with Lysimachus correctly. Conventionally we expect to see a demonstration of Marina's reputation, and possibly we hope to see Marina defeat him as she has done all the other clients.

The Bawd does her best to recommend Marina, knowing full well how awkward that might prove: 'We have here one, sir, if she would – but there never came her like in Mytilene' (ll. 26–7). Her failure to complete her sentence is picked up by Lysimachus who finishes it for her, adding 'If she'd do the deeds of darkness, thou wouldst say' (ll. 28–9). Put this together with his opening remark, and his comment about the health of prostitutes and clients, and it is clear that Lysimachus's visit is expressly for Marina, the recently advertised virgin. His impatience is evident – 'Well, call forth, call forth' (l. 31) – but when Boult also fails to finish a sentence (l. 34), just as coyly as his mistress the Bawd, Lysimachus this time fails to join in the game and instead demands, 'What, prithee?' (l. 35). As a contraction of 'I pray thee', this polite formality places Boult's assumed coyness in sharp perspective. Lysimachus has had enough of the banter and especially of their pretence to decency. He knows that Boult was going to continue 'and she were a rose indeed, if she had but –' with the idiomatic 'a prick'. When instead, like the Bawd, he replies with more feigned coyness, 'O, sir, I can be modest' (l. 36), Lysimachus finally shows some signs of the nobility and decency which he must demonstrate if he is to become a suitable husband for Marina:

> That dignifies the renown of a bawd no less than it gives a good report to a number to be chaste. [*Exit Boult.*]
>
> (4.vi.37–8)

Lysimachus exposes both the Bawd's and Boult's attempts at modesty for the ridiculous pretences they are, and perhaps the Bawd takes his hint since as Marina enters, she eschews any further coyness and reverts to the kind of language she normally uses with Boult and her husband:

> Here comes that which grows to the stalk; never pluck'd yet, I can assure you.
>
> (4.vi.39–40)

The final exchange of this first section raises a fascinating question for a director of the play. How can Marina's entrance and her reception by Lysimachus be staged?

The Bawd's question is direct and simple: 'Is she not a fair creature?' as though she knows that understatement will work best in the presence of the reality. Lysimachus's reply, 'Faith, she would serve after a long voyage at sea' (l. 42), is the key to this question. It is obviously sardonic and is made to keep the Bawd's ambitious claims under control, which is why it is also followed immediately by his making a payment, 'Well, there's for you; leave us' (l. 43). There is also a bleak irony in the form his reply takes considering Marina's history and ties with the sea. But what is most evident is that his reply is made after he has regarded Marina. It cannot be otherwise. It is likely that Lysimachus is struck instantly by Marina's beauty and his sardonic reply only highlights that. There is no further debate. The pleasantries cease when Lysimachus sees what he came for and the bargain is made, but such is the Bawd's fear of Marina's power that she asks leave to speak to her before departing.

Aside, the Bawd speaks directly to Marina in an attempt to make sure she will permit Lysimachus to take her virginity. It is quite shrewd of her to start by telling Marina Lysimachus is 'an honourable man'. Marina's reply is circumspect, 'I desire to find him so, that I may worthily note him' (ll. 49–50), yet polite enough to allow the Bawd some hope. The Bawd adds that not only is he 'the governor of this country' (l. 51) but she is 'bound to him' (l. 52). Marina acknowledges his claim to respect as governor but reserves judgement on his honour, which so clearly rests on his behaviour towards her. The confidence Marina displays shifts the Bawd's tone from controlled appeasement to blunt anger:

> Pray you, without any more virginal fencing, will you use him kindly? He will line your apron with gold.
>
> (4.vi.56–8)

Marina maintains her air of confident chastity by going only as far as to promise to 'thankfully receive' (l. 59) whatever Lysimachus cares to 'do graciously'. The Bawd's time runs out when Lysimachus's impatience shows itself, 'Ha' you done?' (l. 61), but she tries to ensure his success by appealing then to his estimation of his own experience in crudely familiar terms which again debase Marina by comparing her to an unbroken horse:

> My lord, she's not pac'd yet; you must take some pains to work her to your manage.
>
> (4.vi.62–3)

In the Jacobean world, patience and physical strength would have been the accepted tools required to break a horse, and the Bawd knows that Marina, like an unruly filly, will not succumb easily. Trusting to Lysimachus's previous experience in the saddle, she then instructs her husband and Boult to leave him alone with Marina, which brings us to Marina's triumphant conversion of Lysimachus from lust to chastened admiration.

Following the Bawd's advice, Lysimachus begins his attempt on Marina's virginity with what appears to be polite conversation, but it involves a very curious question, 'Now, pretty one, how long have you been at this trade?' (ll. 64–5). This is curious because he has already paid for a virgin. We are faced with two alternatives here. Either Lysimachus distrusts the Bawd completely and doesn't believe Marina is a virgin at all, which runs counter to earlier remarks he has made, though it smacks of realism, or he is simply a bit of a bungler when it comes to seduction. It is hardly tactful to address a naive young girl, the unschooled filly described by the Bawd, as a whore, in the first breath. But if we examine the exchange as it develops, Lysimachus actually uses quite a rich array of euphemisms such as 'trade', 'profession', 'gamester' and 'creature of sale' where the audience might reasonably expect a straightforward 'whore'. When prompted by Marina to speak his mind, 'What trade, sir?' (l. 67), 'Please you to name it' (ll. 69–70), he cannot bring himself to use the precise word and fences, coyly. Only moments ago we saw him do exactly the same to the Bawd and Boult, exposing their hypocrisy as he did so. By directly paralleling Marina's use of language with Lysimachus's, Shakespeare makes her appear superior from the moment their conversation begins, and guides it deftly to the point where she exposes his hypocrisy just as effectively as he did the Bawd's or Boult's:

> Do you know this house to be a place of such resort, and will come into't?
>
> (4.vi.78–9)

In spite of all we have discovered so far, the whole business of Marina's invulnerable virginity and her astonishing habit of turning customers into converts, remains problematic for contemporary audiences. Lysimachus's transformation from frequenter of brothels to noble suitor happens at break-neck speed and consequently perturbs our appetite for realism. Yet the scene is written (with one exception we will examine later) to make complete dramatic sense. Lysimachus is outwitted by Marina as soon as he opens his mouth, and his essentially moral character exploited by her wit. When he asks her, 'How long have you been of this profession?' (l. 71), her 'E'er since I can remember' (l. 72) is a clever piece of ambiguity since Marina is thinking of the only 'profession' she knows, that of being virtuous. But her apparent admission shocks even 'the lewdly-inclin'd' Lysimachus and his attempt to seduce is nowhere to be seen in his outraged response,

> Did you go to't so young? Were you a gamester at five or at seven?
>
> (4.vi.73–4)

Marina's evasive wit puzzles Lysimachus further, 'Earlier too, sir, if now I be one' (l. 75), and he can only stumble after her with a kind of crude logic,

> Why, the house you dwell in proclaims you to be a creature of sale
>
> (4.vi.76–7)

into the trap she has laid. There is no repudiating the question she then poses and if this were verse we were analysing, we would be able to point to a caesura in line 79 which would underline his inability to respond. However, although this is prose, it does not exclude the possibility that Marina's speech here contains a complete break. She waits for an answer when she asks, 'Do you know this house to be a place of such resort, and will come into't?' (l. 79), but when one doesn't come, she continues with a wholly new tactic. 'I hear say you're of honourable parts and are the governor of this place' (ll. 79–80).

To the new information, Lysimachus can respond, and he does so in a predictably masculine and defensive manner, demanding to know if the Bawd has told Marina who he is. His anger is clear when Marina evades his question with 'Who is my principal?' (l. 83). If we consider his response, the anger is evident even in the first word. 'Why' is not a question. It indicates impatience, as though he does not believe her when she denies knowing; it means something closer to 'For God's sake' or 'Don't pretend you don't know.' This is absolutely understandable when we consider how deftly Marina has just manoeuvred Lysimachus into staring his own hypocrisy in the face. Anger seems present, too, in his description of the Bawd as 'she that sets seeds and roots of shame and iniquity' (ll. 84–5), and in the exclamatory,

O, you have heard something of my power, and so stand aloof
for more serious wooing.

(4.vi.85–6)

As yet wholly unable to see Marina as the audience does, Lysimachus
suspects she is merely seeking more money and using delay and
frustration as the means to get it. Consequently he adopts a more
threatening tone,

But I protest to thee, pretty one, my authority shall not see thee,
or else look friendly upon thee.

(4.vi.87–9)

Lysimachus reminds Marina that she is so insignificant as to be
beneath his concern as governor. He will neither 'see' her, that is
acknowledge her existence as a prostitute, 'or else' (or otherwise)
'look friendly' (l. 88) on her, treat her kindly. He has tried patience
and failed, so now he has to try strength. Lysimachus has had enough
of her pretence, he believes her to be as corrupt as the Bawd, and his
lust moves him to act:

Come, bring me to some private place; come, come.

(4.vi.89–90)

The repetition of 'come' and the imperative 'bring', combined
with Marina's outright plea for kindness, suggest that Lysimachus
has physically taken hold of Marina and is close to considering
rape:

If you were born to honour, show it now;
If put upon you, make the judgement good
That thought you worthy of it.

(4.vi.91–3)

Her appeal to his sense of nobility and 'honour', the consistent theme
of her dialogue with him, now abandons witty brevity for an eloquently balanced expression that gives him just enough pause for

thought. Whether he was born honourable or has been the recipient
of honour, in either case Marina pleads with him to prove himself
worthy by relinquishing his lustful intent.

Lysimachus shows he is both confused, 'How's this? how's this?',
and as yet unconvinced, 'Some more; be sage' (l. 93), where the latter
expression seems deliberately ambiguous. Marina is advised to either
make good her demand by further speech, or be sensible and give
herself up to him.

Marina's defence here is possibly the most problematic section of
the whole play. This is the point referred to earlier, where the
dramatic sense dramatically fails. It is clear that the text here is very
corrupt, and although any good edition of the play will discuss the
various reasons and possible causes, they will also point out the
impossibility of reconstruction. (Marina's defence of her virginity
when Boult attempts to rape her at the end of the scene is much
lengthier and far less significant.) We even have the tantalising
reply from Lysimachus to draw our attention to the loss of this
speech:

> I did not think
> Thou couldst have spoke so well; ne'er dreamt thou couldst.
> Had I brought hither a corrupted mind,
> Thy speech had alter'd it.
>
> (4.vi.101–4)

However eloquently Marina spoke, whatever poetry she used to
make Lysimachus say this and transform him into her suitor, there
remains only the outer shell. The first three lines seem the start of a
lengthy sentence, broken after 'physic' (l. 97), though Marina's sense
of outrage is already strongly conveyed in the image of the brothel as
a 'sty' (l. 96) and in the notion that 'Diseases have been sold dearer
than physic' (l. 97). The remaining four lines voice her desperate
desire for liberty but in terms which bind it inseparably to the whole
question of honour and virtue:

> That the gods
> Would set me free from this unhallow'd place,

Though they did change me to the meanest bird
That flies i'th' purer air!

(4.vi.98–101)

In her wish to be free as a bird, Marina also yearns for the clean,
'purer' air.

We might surmise a little of the content from combining Marina's
use of 'That the gods' (l. 98) and 'The good gods preserve thee!'
(l. 107), with Lysimachus's words:

Persever in that clear way though goest,
And the good gods strengthen thee!

(4.vi.105–6)

Shakespeare's use of imagery is skilful and controlled, so it is likely
that both the gods, and imagery involving purity and clarity, figured
strongly in her defence.

Before he departs, the degree of Lysimachus's conversion is very
clear. He denies entering the brothel with 'ill intent' (l. 109), by which
he appears to mean cruelty rather than sinfulness, and he aligns
himself with Marina by building on her descriptive imagery for the
brothel, claiming 'The very doors and windows savour vilely' (l. 110).
Her virtue he sees as proof of her nobility,

Thou art a piece of virtue, and
I doubt not but thy training hath been noble.

(4.vi.111–12)

which prompts him to give her more gold, since money is the one
thing he can provide her with that might help her defend herself, as
proves the case when she buys Boult's rape attempt off (4.vi.180).
Assuring her of his future assistance,

If thou dost
Hear from me, it shall be for thy good.

(4.vi.115–16)

he is interrupted by Boult's untimely entry and request for payment, 'I beseech your honour, one piece for me' (l. 117), which permits his explosive exit, as dramatic a contrast to his entrance as one could wish:

> Avaunt thou damned door-keeper! Your house,
> But for this virgin that doth prop it,
> Would sink and overwhelm you all. Away!
> (4.vi.118–120)

It is doubly ironic that he uses the same sea imagery in connection with Marina which he employed far less charitably when trying to buy her earlier in the scene (l. 42).

Marina has survived one of the most demanding, seemingly impossible tests any of Shakespeare's heroines have to endure. It is a sad loss that the core of her defence did not survive in the text as well.

Time and Tide

The passage of time is extremely significant in all four of the late plays. At one end of the scale we have *The Tempest*, which appears to have a very classical approach to time, all the action taking place in one twenty-four-hour period. At the other extreme are *The Winter's Tale* and *Pericles*, where it is roughly the sixteen years it takes for Perdita and Marina to reach marriageable age that frames the action. In *Cymbeline*, the action takes place over an unspecified period governed by the time it takes Iachimo and Posthumus to journey between Rome and Britain, and Imogen and Cloten to travel to Wales. Nonetheless, the time needed to allow the abducted princes Arviragus and Belarius to grow up is important, and even in *The Tempest*, Prospero's auspicious star accords with Miranda's reaching nubility. What this points to is the absolutely central concern in all four plays with the family, reconciliation and regeneration.

Shakespeare exploits time for both dramatic as well as ideological ends, and unusually in *Pericles*, he employs a choric figure, the medi-

aeval poet John Gower, who in some ways functions like the only
other significant choral figure in Shakespeare, the chorus in *Henry V*.
Gower provides both the prologue and epilogue, appears between
acts and not only presents the action but at times interprets it for us.
One of the key functions both choral figures have is to explain away
the passage of time. This is what we find Gower doing at the start of
Act 4.

Even a cursory glance at the printed page should be enough to tell
us that the lines are generally shorter than is usual. Gower also uses
rhyming couplets throughout, something we find far more frequently
in Shakespeare's earlier plays than in these late plays. The first thing
we need to do is explain this disparity. Why has Shakespeare differentiated Gower's verse in this way? A glance at the names sprinkled
throughout his speech, Tyre, Ephesus, Tharsus, Cleon, Philoten,
shows us that the archaic, ancient tone of the whole tale was as
ancient and enigmatic, historically, to Shakespeare's audience as it is
to us. Shakespeare is eager to enforce the tone he would have found
in his romance sources, of an ancient tale based on a half mythical
world rooted vaguely in classical Greece. The opening lines of the
play are

> To sing a song that old was sung,
> From ashes ancient Gower is come,
> (1.i.1–2)

and they quite cleverly distance the story doubly from the audience.
Not only is this resurrected Gower 'ancient' himself, but the tale is far
older than him. Gower continues his opening chorus,

> To glad your ear, and please your eyes.
> It hath been sung at festivals,
> On ember-eves and holy-ales;
> And lords and ladies in their lives
> Have read it for restoratives:
> The purchase is to make men glorious,
> Et bonum quo antiquius eo melius.
> (1.i.4–10)

which is as clear a guide as anyone could wish for, when it comes to the play's overall dramatic effect. Any director who ignores this injunction is walking a very fine wire indeed. Shakespeare's hope is that his audience leave the theatre restored, enriched and imbued with a profound faith in man as a divine creation. It is a bold intention. (The Latin maxim can be translated as, 'And the older a good thing is, the better.')

It appears then, that Gower is primarily there to give the tale gravity, the gravity of time. Shakespeare therefore attempts to make Gower's verse appropriately mediaeval, something even more obvious in the earlier acts than in the later ones.

It is also worth a slight digression here to highlight the stress Gower places on 'To glad your ear', which comes before 'and please your eyes' (l. 4). It is a timely reminder that Shakespeare's audience lived primarily in an aural, not a visual culture, which is one reason why verse analysis of the type dominant in this study is an appropriate critical approach. Having understood why Gower's verse differs, we can now turn our attention to what he says, and to our central analytical question, how did, or might, this work on stage?

In the opening four lines of Act 4 we find him settling our curiosity about both Pericles and Thaisa with ruthless efficiency and with the invitation to 'Imagine' (l. 1). The former is welcomed home and the latter sadly resigned to life as a priestess to Diana. It is Marina we are now going to be concerned with. Gower says, 'Now to Marina bend your mind' (l. 4), again inviting us to engage our imaginations before the actors enter. His acknowledgement of the artifice, 'Whom our fast-growing scene must find' (l. 6), is, as in *Henry V*, quite a sophisticated theatrical device because it depends on the audience being able to slide in and out of their suspension of disbelief at will. At the beginning of each act, when the ancient and possibly very distinguishable figure of Gower makes his entrance, the audience has to quickly ease itself out of the action involving Pericles and his family, and pay attention to this narrator, whose very presence exposes the dramatic artifice of the other actors, while his speech reminds them that the entire proceedings rely on his telling. Yet he is of course another actor, strongly differentiated from their era by his speech and costume, which entails a different suspension of disbelief.

We may even see something of Prospero in Gower, in this godlike control of others. The aura of magic would certainly have been appropriate for such a 'mouldy tale'.

Once he has drawn our attention to Marina, Gower then eulogises her while simultaneously driving the plot forward through his description of the hapless Philoten, and of Dionyza's murderous envy. The first of Marina's accomplishments mentioned, not surprisingly in a play that places such weight on it, is music. In time she

> hath gain'd
> Of education all the grace,
> Which makes her both the heart and place
> Of general wonder.
> (4.i.9–11)

Although this is praise indeed, Gower's eulogy gains even greater heights as he portrays Marina's life in Tharsus. A caesura marks the shift in tone from admiration and awe to dark foreboding. Marina is the object of murderous envy and Cleon's daughter, Philoten, the apparently innocent cause. Gower notes that Philoten 'Would ever with Marina be' (4.i.20) and describes them pursuing conventional feminine activities together, in each case Marina's skill far outshining Philoten's. This picture of the perfect Marina, companioned by the inadequate Philoten, occupies Gower for sixteen lines (ll. 17–33) and is written as one, long, gently lyrical sentence employing soft vowel sounds to match the beauty of the intimate scenes Gower conjures for us. Gower praises Marina's skill in sewing via a very contemporary conceit which relies on paradox for its effect. The wounding of the material with her needle only makes the cloth 'more sound / By hurting it' (ll. 24–5), an image Donne would have leapt on. Marina sings even more beautifully than the nightingale, and her innocent purity is enforced by the image of her writing to the goddess Diana 'with rich and constant pen' (l. 28). Gower's idyllic, pastoral scenes are, however, superbly undermined by the final damning image of Philoten competing with Marina,

> So
> With dove of Paphos might the crow
> Vie feathers white.
>
> (4.i.31–3)

Coming as it does after such a long, lyrical description, this terse
dismissal simultaneously eulogises Marina and provides us with a
powerful reason for her imminent danger.

This envy between half-sisters, or more precisely, between stepmother and stepdaughter, is of course a fundamental folk motif. Yet
categorising it as such runs the risk of underestimating its significance. Whether Shakespeare was conscious of using it as a motif or
not does not negate the terrible truth it reveals. Horrifying as it may
be, even today a stepchild is statistically at great risk from its step-
parent.

Gower has been alone on stage for some time now, but Shakespeare has divided his potentially dull soliloquy into clearly delineated
sections, using rhythm to control our response. The harsh curtness of

> But, alack,
> That monster envy, oft the wrack
> Of earned praise,
>
> (4.i.11–12)

contrasts sharply with the soft fluency of lines 17 to 33, ending as we
have noted in the sudden undermining of Philoten. From that point
the rhythm is once more dominated by determined, strong conson-
ants, where 'gets', 'debts', 'darks' and 'marks' establish a more rigid
rhyme which is backed up later by 'stead' and 'dead'. We learn of
Dionyza's plot to kill Marina and that the death of Marina's nurse,
Lychorida, has made such a plot easier. But a caesura in line 45 puts
an end to the ominous tone as Gower resumes his role as chorus
openly, in a much more familiar, friendly, relaxed manner:

> The unborn event
> I do commend to your content;
> Only I carried winged time

Post on the lame feet of my rime;
Which never could I so convey,
Unless your thoughts went on my way.
(4.i.45–50)

His appeal is gentle and unassuming, politely apologetic, but at the same time wholly conscious of the nature of the audience's illusion. Finally, Shakespeare eschews all artifice and makes Gower announce Dionyza and Leonine like some festive master of ceremonies before he exits to leave us free to engage with the newcomers, honed as we are with foreknowledge of their intent:

Dionyza does appear,
With Leonine, a murtherer.
(4.i.51–2)

What is potentially a highly undramatic speech and moment in the drama, Shakespeare divides and manipulates to ensure that the audience is never allowed to lose interest. A relationship between time and plot is integral to all but the most avant garde drama but in these plays it is also deeply rooted in the family and in ideas of regeneration.

Suffering and Forgiveness

One of the most effective, common features of these plays is their supreme articulation of human suffering. Hermione in *The Winter's Tale* is made to endure quite appalling misery, emotional and even physical, while Pericles seems to be victimised by some evil deity intent on destroying his every happiness the moment he finds it. Imogen's absolute fidelity in *Cymbeline* she sees hurled back in her face as lust, while Prospero in *The Tempest* is cast adrift in a boat with a baby daughter and his books to keep him company. But if there is intense suffering in these plays there is also quite astounding forgiveness.

In the hands of a competent director and cast, the reconciliation between Pericles and Marina (5.i.) is undoubtedly one of the most moving scenes Shakespeare ever wrote. It is well worth asking what contributes directly to its reputation as an emotional experience in the theatre. Pericles is on a barge, hidden from view at the start of the scene. It is an interesting example of how even simple staging issues, such as where the characters actually physically stand and move in relationship to each other, can have considerable influence on dramatic effect.

The scene contains some enticing stage directions and there are a number of points to make about visualising it as a performance. Although the Globe theatre had a balcony which was used to stage action in some way separated from the action below on the main platform, it seems extremely unlikely that this scene used that balcony, as Lysimachus and Marina move readily from Pericles' inner position, to a space removed sufficiently to allow the illusion of privacy, but not so far as to involve any journey time. But even more persuasive than this is the fact that the whole scene is one of such emotional power and impact that anything which physically distances the audience from it (such as raising it back and up onto the balcony) would restrict its success. It seems much more likely that Pericles was hidden behind a curtain of some kind, even centre stage, and that once it was drawn back, Marina and the others moved to and from him to indicate whether or not they were within his hearing.

Lysimachus sees Marina approach as he is speaking to Helicanus about Pericles, and immediately refers, twice, to her beauty:

> Welcome, fair one! Is't not a goodly presence?
> (5.i.65)

When Helicanus agrees, Lysimachus admits that if he could be assured Marina were well born, he would think himself fortunate to marry her. As it would be entirely inappropriate for Marina to hear this, it must be that the first part of his speech (ll. 67–9) is delivered only to Helicanus, and his subsequent appeal to Marina to aid Pericles, more publicly. There is clearly dramatic sense here in the idea that Lysimachus should appear so in love with Marina, since part of the reconciliation will involve their betrothal.

Marina accepts the task asked of her, on the condition that everyone except her and her 'companion maid' withdraw, which seems to be a dramatic device to concentrate all our attention on the reconciliation itself, while keeping the element of music by having a musician stay with Marina in the shape of her maid servant. With the other characters at a safe distance, and Pericles suitably costumed and positioned to appear utterly insensible and unapproachable, Marina sings. As with so many Shakespearean songs, this one is lost, but we should not totally abandon thinking about it because of that. Music is used purposefully in this play, frequently as an accompaniment to healing, and in association with ideals of female beauty. It is safe therefore to assume that the song would have been designed to impress the audience with its beauty and power to move them, so that Pericles' absolute immobility is both dramatically shocking and disappointing. Marina has to be asked by Lysimachus whether or not Pericles responded and she replies with a firm negative, 'No, nor look'd on us' (l. 80). Only when Marina speaks to him does Pericles respond at all and with a barely human sound Shakespeare renders as 'Hum, ha!' (l. 83), adding the inhuman action *pushing her back*. To an audience steeped in everything from the polite rules and gestures of common courtesy to the elaborate etiquette of the court, this moment must have been far more shocking than it might be today. That Marina, too, conceives of his action as an insult is clear from the words 'I am a maid' (l. 84), and the image she uses to open her appeal to him. Her avowal that she has never invited looks, yet has 'been gaz'd on like a comet' (l. 86), reminds us once more of the great potency physical beauty has in this play. It would be interesting, for example, to consider in some detail what part physical beauty plays in Marina's life and in the life of Antiochus's daughter. Marina appears to refer to it to make sure Pericles does not misunderstand her present role, but her assurance that she may have undergone as much grief as him is what initiates the possibility of recognition in the minds of the audience:

> She speaks,
> My lord, that, may be, hath endur'd a grief
> Might equal yours, if both were justly weigh'd.
>
> (5.i.86–8)

Marina's suggestion that she might understand his grief penetrates Pericles' shell of misery sufficiently for him to pick up some of her words. When she refers directly to her 'parentage' and regal ancestry, the poignancy of the dramatic situation is driven home.

Part of Shakespeare's art in these plays is his ability to tease out dramatic irony to perfection and this scene is possibly the supreme example of that. The audience has known, from the moment Lysimachus mentioned her, that, ignorant of the fact, Marina would be about to see her father for the first time. The possibility of their recognising each other is further hampered by Pericles' state of insensible grief. Now, that irony is given voice, and in Marina's complaint the audience hears precisely what it wants to hear. But Shakespeare teases the moment out to its limit by having her interrupt herself at the caesura in line 94 – 'I will desist' – before putting words into her mouth which introduce an element of mystery into the proceedings and appeal to our uniquely human instinct for the joy that comes from observing patience rewarded and suffering cease:

> But there is something glows upon my cheek,
> And whispers in mine ear 'Go not till he speak'.
> (5.i.95–6)

Pericles then begins to speak, in halting words that reveal precisely what it is in her speech that has dragged him out of his stupor. Not for the first time the Gordian ties of the family are at the heart of the drama, and as Marina responds, Pericles takes a step closer to recognition by looking at her and, we assume, seeing something to resemble Thaisa in her features, 'You're like something that' (5.i. 102). But it is his reference to 'shores' which gives Marina the cue to provide a clue to her identity, which Pericles is as yet still too stunned to comprehend, further exploiting dramatic irony since the audience understands her riddle, 'No, nor of any shores' (5.i.103), only too well.

Shakespeare then provides Pericles with the most reverberatingly ironic image of all in this scene, by casting him in the role of a mother giving birth:

> I am great with woe
> And shall deliver weeping.
>
> (5.i.105–6)

and permitting him to voice what his eyes have been telling him, that the girl before him is not only like his wife, but like his daughter might have been. Skilfully, the focus of our attention has shifted; it is Marina now who is the chief object of the dramatic irony, and in her matter-of-fact replies, she shows her lack of comprehension clearly:

> Where I am but a stranger; from the deck
> You may discern the place.
>
> (5.i.114–15)

This ekes out the moment of recognition even further since Marina, having accomplished her task in making Pericles speak, has no further need to prolong this conversation beyond the urgency imposed on her by Pericles. It is his grief she has been requested to ease, not her own, and when he asks her to recount her life story she quite understandably avoids doing so:

> If I should tell my history, 'twould seem
> Like lies, disdain'd in the reporting.
>
> (5.i.118–19)

Having raised the possibility of Marina telling her story, Shakespeare frustrates her, prolonging the emotional power of the scene, by making Pericles employ a kind of urgent persuasion in which, while trying to convince her that he will believe her, he simultaneously prevents her from speaking. He asks, 'What were thy friends?' (l. 124), only to interrupt her reply of 'So indeed I did' (l. 128) with further demands. In his haste to know, Pericles prevents his knowing.

But perhaps the absolute masterstroke of dramaturgy comes after Shakespeare has calmed Pericles down and given us every indication that Marina will reveal her true identity in a narrative of her life. 'Tell thy story,' Pericles says, as though they are to share each others' sufferings in some competition to see whose life has been most painful:

> If thine consider'd prove the thousandth part
> Of my endurance, thou art a man, and I
> Have suffer'd like a girl.
>
>   (5.i.135–7)

As though alert at last to his own haste, he employs an understandably famous image to describe Marina's composed beauty:

>   yet thou dost look
> Like Patience gazing on kings' graves, and smiling
> Extremity out of act.
>
>   (5.i.137–9)

Once again a caesura is used to break up the speech. Possibly Pericles is meant to gaze on Marina, entranced, before excitement at the prospect of her tale makes him utter the crop of short, single-sentence questions which follow:

>   What were thy friends?
> How lost thou them? Thy name, most kind virgin?
>   (5.i.139–40)

Pericles is given the chance to recover himself, and in a calmer, rhythmically controlled single line, he gives every indication, in verse and gesture, that Marina's tale is about to begin, 'Recount, I do beseech you. Come, sit by me' (l. 141).

Shakespeare's masterstroke is to have Marina answer the single most pertinent of Pericles' former questions, instead of beginning her tale. Her deliciously simple 'My name is Marina' (5.i.142) explodes with a huge emotional impact on the audience, and on Pericles too, whose emotional reaction is strong enough to make Marina consider speaking no further.

Substantial effort has gone into making this moment as powerful as possible because it marks both the culmination of Pericles' suffering and, paradoxically, his reward. Shakespeare's vision is of a world in which patience is indeed a virtue, and if there is such a thing, balance the ordering principle. Diana's appearance to Pericles in the dream which ends the scene, and her instruction to him to visit her temple at Ephesus to recount his trials, is merely the formal signification of his ability to forgive. In forgiving the anonymous, inimical force which destroyed his joys, Pericles' reward is as intense as his suffering.

Divine Magic

Probably the most frustrating aspect of the late plays for students and audiences today is their ready acceptance of the use of magic and divine intervention. In a predominantly godless society, which yet regards itself as godlike in its apparently unlimited application of science and technology, even to the fundamental processes of creation, there is little space for Cerimon and Apollo, Prospero and Jupiter. If we are to understand Shakespeare's use of magic in these plays, we have to start by appreciating at least a little of the Jacobean view in this respect. Primarily, God was simply not an issue. The great struggles at the heart of most European nations between Catholic and Protestant ideologies, which dominated this historical period, penetrated to the caves of even the most obscure hermits. Belief in God was literally a matter of life or death for many people. It is not a very difficult step from belief in a Christian God, and his antithesis, Satan, to a belief in the power of magic. King James I himself wrote a scholarly book on magic, and one has only to think of the havoc wreaked by magic in Salem, Massachusetts, adroitly exploited by Arthur Miller in *The Crucible*, to realise that a Jacobean audience would regard the magical moments and episodes in the late plays untroubled by any kind of scepticism or doubt. What doubts they do have are moral ones.

In Act 3 of *Pericles*, the enigmatic Cerimon is as much healer as magician, as is evident when he calls to his servant Philemon to fetch some basic things, 'fire and meat' (3.ii.2), which will provide comfort for his visitors since they have endured the same terrible storm as Pericles. The first visitor expresses surprise to find Cerimon, a man with all the trappings of wealth, out of bed so early. But his surprise is rhetorical. Both he and his companion know Cerimon's reputation as a kind and generous healer, and the comment about his early rising allows them to compliment him:

> 'Tis most strange,
> Nature should be so conversant with pain,
> Being thereto not compell'd.
>   (3.ii.24–6)

It is also the cue for Cerimon to give his own impeccable credentials. He begins by explaining his philosophy. 'Virtue and cunning' are things he prizes above 'nobleness and riches', since the latter may be wasted by 'careless heirs', while 'immortality attends the former / Making a man a god' (ll. 29–30). It is important to note that 'cunning' carries no negative connotations here, but means something more akin to 'wisdom' or 'intelligence'. His aspiration towards deification is equally positive because it is his skill in handling sickness and injury, the frailty of human life, which is going to be called upon in a moment, not some kind of Faustian ambition. He recounts how, like Friar Lawrence in *Romeo and Juliet*, he has studied medicine, 'physic', and how through hard study, 'turning o'er authorities', and through experience, 'Together with my practice', he has come to understand 'the blest infusions / That dwell in vegetives, in metals, stones' (ll. 35–6). That 'blest' is absolutely vital. Friar Lawrence is self-evidently a Christian. Cerimon inhabits an exotic pre-Christian past, so with him comes an assurance for the audience that he is, like Friar Lawrence, free of any taint of witchcraft. His essential virtue is underpinned in the conclusion of his speech where he once again denounces riches and fame in favour of the 'delight' and 'content' gained in pursuit of his calling.

And if there were any doubt remaining about his impeccable morality, the Second Gentleman produces another testimonial, this time specifically raising the idea that amongst his skills is the ability to restore grievously ill people to good health:

and hundreds call themselves
Your creatures, who by you have been restor'd.
(3.ii.44–5)

This amiable exchange amongst friends is interrupted by the arrival of more servants with an object the audience would instantly suspect, since it is only a matter of minutes ago that they heard the sailor tell Pericles they had a chest 'caulked and bitumed ready' to receive Thaisa's corpse. Cerimon uses the same term exactly, 'How close 'tis caulked and bitumed!' (l. 57), to make the connection even more explicit, before the lid is prised off and Thaisa's unconscious form revealed. The conventional tokens confirm her identity before Cerimon's assertion that her 'burial' has only just taken place: 'This chanc'd tonight' (3.ii.79), impels us on to the next obvious step. Noting 'how fresh she looks', Cerimon concludes 'They were too rough / That threw her in the sea' (ll. 81–2) and urgently requests a servant to bring a fire and 'all my boxes in my closet'.

Once the servant returns with the necessary items, Cerimon calls for the music, which in these plays frequently has both a medicinal and an aesthetic function. Whatever actions now take place, they are in a sense peripheral because the expectation that Thaisa is alive has been placed in the audience's mind ever since the chest appeared, if not earlier. Some of Cerimon's words may indicate urgency or impatience: 'How thou stirr'st, thou block!' which could be admonishing a servant, and 'The music there!' which comes after he has already requested the music for a second time, and finally 'I pray you, give her air', which precedes the miraculous 'Gentlemen, this queen will live' (l. 94). In such a situation, a sense of excitement and urgency is only natural, and would contrast effectively with Thaisa's awakening, which cannot really be staged other than slowly and gradually. Cerimon suggests this himself, 'Nature awakes a warm breath out of her' (l. 95) and 'See how she 'gins to blow into life's flower again!' (l. 97). He then describes how her eyes open, through a conceit that can easily confuse because of the rare use of a meaning for the word 'water':

Behold, her eyelids, cases to those
Heavenly jewels which Pericles has lost,

Begin to part their fringes of bright gold.
The diamonds of a most praised water
Doth appear to make the world twice rich.

                    (3.ii.100–4)

As so often in plays of the period, poetry serves to convey what eyes
cannot see, and as the small group of watchers peer entranced, while
Thaisa's presumably supine body stirs, Shakespeare puts what they
see into Cerimon's mouth. It is a pretty, though not especially original
metaphor to make eyes jewels and eyelashes 'fringes of bright gold'.
But there is deeper poignancy when we extend the jewel metaphor to
Thaisa herself. Her father, Simonides, had presented her to the
competing knights with these words:

                    our daughter,
In honour of whose birth these triumphs are,
Sits here like Beauty's child, whom Nature gat
For men to see, and seeing wonder at.

                    (2.ii.4–7)

and when Thaisa modestly denies the praise, he adds:

It's fit it should be so; for princes are
A model which heaven makes like to itself:
As jewels lose their glory if neglected,
So princes their renowns if not respected.

                    (2.ii.10–13)

It is clear Thaisa is a 'jewel' Pericles has lost. But it is the latter part of
the speech which contains the potential for confusion. The word
'water' when applied to jewellery can mean 'lustre', and Cerimon's
'diamonds of most praised water', although superficially describing
Thaisa's eyes, refers also to her person, which has been praised in the
passport Cerimon read aloud a moment earlier.

    Interwoven into this action are a number of seemingly innocuous
comments from the gentlemen, which reinforce the aura of magic.
The First Gentleman says,

The heavens, through you, increase our wonder,
And set up your fame forever.

(3.ii.98–9)

and replies 'Most rare' when his companion asks, 'Is not most
strange?' However skilled a healer Cerimon is, the gentlemen clearly
believe what they have just witnessed to be something that is beyond
the knowledge and powers of this world and partakes of the divine.
The gods are seen to be working through Cerimon, just as Apollo
uses Paulina in *The Winter's Tale,* and, as we shall see later in this
chapter, Jupiter interferes to save Posthumus. In the late plays, magic
is always divine. Whether Shakespeare is using Greek gods like
Apollo, as in *The Winter's Tale,* and Diana in *Pericles;* or Roman
gods, like Jupiter in *Cymbeline;* or a mixture of the two like Juno,
Ceres and Iris, as in *The Tempest,* magic is their *modus operandi.* Even
the godlike Prospero links his magical power to the gods and to
'divine providence'. There is no magic in the late plays to rival the
calculated evil of the witches in *Macbeth.*

Revived Families

In this final section on *Pericles,* we will examine the moment when
Shakespeare reunites the family he has taken such elaborate pains to
disassemble. The idea that the late plays form a meaningfully coherent group within the Shakespeare canon has provoked considerable
critical debate, but if there is one thing which they have fundamentally in common, it is a fascination with the family. Blood kinship has
a far stronger significance than merely being a common factor in the
sources Shakespeare used, and one of the aims of this introductory
study is to explore the link between the family and the dramatic
effects of the plays.

Pericles and Marina are reunited with Thaisa at the Temple of
Diana at Ephesus. But where does Shakespeare place the dramatic
weight of this scene? Which of the reconciliations, husband with
wife, or daughter with mother, is given most of his attention? This
question isn't a particularly difficult one to answer. Virtually all the

writing is invested in Pericles and Thaisa, while Marina's delight at
meeting her mother for the first time is merely sketched.

Only a 20-line chorus by Gower (5.ii) separates the reconciliation
scene between Pericles and Marina on the barge from this scene in
Ephesus. The audience has very recently experienced the intense
emotion of the earlier reconciliation. Gower's chorus serves not
only to excuse the real time necessary for Pericles to journey from
Mytilene to Ephesus, but more importantly to ease the audience's
emotional involvement. We have seen how much care went into the
teasing out of that reconciliation, how skilfully Shakespeare exploited
the fundamental situation for dramatic effect, and it is inconceivable
that he could repeat that again immediately. The audience has to be
lulled into a calmer state of mind to prepare for the renewed
emotional intensity of the final scene. The timing is crucial. Shakespeare has engaged the audience's emotions at a high level and a
complete scene or lengthy diversion would necessitate his having to
recover all that. This way he merely disengages the emotion briefly,
calming and soothing us, before tapping back into what he has
already built up.

The stage onto which Pericles and Marina enter is described in full
at the opening of Act 5, Scene iii.

> [*The Temple of Diana at Ephesus;* THAISA *standing near the Altar, as High
> Priestess; a number of Virgins on each Side;* CERIMON *and other Inhabitants of
> Ephesus attending.*]

Into this assembly come 'PERICLES, *with his Train;* LYSIMACHUS,
HELICANUS, *and* MARINA.' The first thing to appreciate is the scale
of this. Besides the six named figures, there are three separate groups:
virgin attendants at the temple; inhabitants of Ephesus accompany-
ing Cerimon; and attendants on Pericles and Marina. This isn't mere
convention. It's a matter of aesthetics. If the audience is to be
brought into the emotional world of the play, and experience a
kind of surrogate emotion akin to the one realised on stage by the
actors, then their role as spectators has to be carefully managed. They
have to be made to feel they are witnesses of this remarkable
spectacle.

Once in place, Pericles wastes no time getting to the point. He begins by announcing his desire to do as Diana's vision instructed him; then, in only a dozen lines, declares his entire history as it relates to Thaisa and Marina. Apart from the reference to Marina's virginity, 'Wears yet thy silver livery' (l. 7), there is really no imagery or description. It is a blunt and objective account, devoid of blame or anger. The reconciliation with Marina has lifted Pericles totally out of his despondent grief and he comes to this altar full of thanks and free from recrimination. Antiochus's murderous plot has become 'frighted from my country' (l. 3). Even Thaisa's death is treated with the neutrality of an historical fact, 'At sea in childbed died she' (l. 5). What matters here is simply that he tells his history so that Thaisa can hear him. By the end of his brief account she faints, and with just enough words to assure the audience she has recognised Pericles: 'Voice and favour! / You are, you are – O royal Pericles!' (ll. 13–14). The curt phrases and repetition all indicate her emotion, and the exchanges between Pericles and Cerimon too which follow, until Thaisa recovers sufficiently to speak, are brief, urgent and extremely simple.

The presence of virgin attendants on Thaisa might suggest that it is they who assist Thaisa during this exchange between Pericles and Cerimon. It certainly appears as though Pericles and Thaisa do not make any physical contact until 'O come, be buried / A second time within these arms' (ll. 44–5), and they are only close enough for her to recognise her father's ring at line 39. It is Cerimon who appears to draw Pericles' attention back to his wife after Cerimon has invited him to his house to view the recognition tokens, 'Look, Thaisa is / Recovered' (ll. 27–8).

When Thaisa speaks, the verse conveys a mixture of disbelief and joy through its shifts in rhythm and address. 'O, let me look!' she exclaims as she comes round, again suggesting perhaps those virgins helping her are barring her view.

If he be none of mine, my sanctity
Will to my sense bend no licentious ear,
But curb it, spite of seeing.
                                        (5.iii.29–31)

This longer, difficult sentence is sandwiched between curt phrases; the rhythm is calmer and the tone more formal, as though she is primarily addressing a public audience. That this is the case appears more likely when we think of it in context and examine the meaning. Thaisa is Diana's high priestess and Diana is the virgin goddess. For her to be fainting over, and stumbling excitedly towards a strange man, is hardly temple etiquette. The point is not a trivial one. Virginity in the late plays is as potent a force for good as fidelity. Thaisa reassures her stage audience, and the real audience, that there is nothing in her behaviour that could cause offence.

After this, she returns to the simple, personal address of emotion, 'O, my lord, / Are you not Pericles?' (ll. 31–2), and what could be less elaborate, less ornate than 'A birth and death?' (l. 34). Pericles, too, responds without gloss or detail, 'The voice of dead Thaisa!' (l. 34). Having taken pains to lead us to it, Shakespeare has the confidence to allow the situation to speak for itself. There is, as a result, something sketchy, hasty or unpolished about this encounter but simultaneously, if properly evoked, something penetratingly powerful on stage. The theatre audience has been invisibly melded into the stage audience, and all the tingling poignancy of the dramatic situation brought home as a result. We feel *with* the family a tiny portion of the real emotion, a pure, untroubled empathy. The astonishment and delight of this scene are feelings not only felt by Pericles, Marina and Thaisa; these joys are public property. That this is the case can easily be seen if we compare this moment of reconciliation with the earlier one between Pericles and Marina. Then, their lengthy, drawn out, gradual discovery of each other was done in private, away from Lysimachus, Helicanus and the others. The theatre audience became privileged voyeurs. How this difference affects the emotion experienced by the audience is a complex question of subtle aesthetics. But deciding which of the two moments Shakespeare may have wished to form the climax of the play might be a start in this direction.

In all of this, Pericles does not neglect to express his appreciation of the gods who have made his 'past miseries sports' (l. 41). 'Immortal Dian!' (l. 37) he exclaims, and in an image reminiscent of his discovery of Marina (5.i.191–4) he voices his joy in touchingly tender terms:

You shall do well,
That on the touching of her lips I may
Melt and no more be seen.

(5.iii.41–3)

The imagery of joy and death is exploited further in his use of 'buried'
(l. 43) and it is a reasonable assumption to make that, as she witnesses
Thaisa and Pericles embrace, Marina is moved to physically respond,
and kneels as she says, 'My heart / Leaps to be gone into my
mother's bosom' (ll. 44–5).

Modern readers might find the absence of naturalistic dialogue at
this point frustrating and even sentimental, but we need to keep a
stage version firmly in mind. It is the image of the family, the *sight* of
their reunion which is so potent. Pericles need only invite Thaisa to
speak to her daughter in acknowledgement, and the two women to
address each other respectfully, for the sight to have the dramatic
impact it needs. Thaisa's ignorance of Helicanus, and Cerimon's
subsequent explanations, are then not only conventional proofs,
but also a means to ease the audience out of the stage audience and
back into the auditorium; an aesthetic response confirmed by
Gower's epilogue.

Pericles is certainly one of Shakespeare's most troubling plays
critically. Attempts have been made to explain it away as experimental; as only partly Shakespeare's; as bridging the gap between the
flawed genius of *Antony and Cleopatra*, and the far more successful *The
Winter's Tale* and *The Tempest*. However disturbing critics find it, in the
hands of skilled theatrical practitioners, knowledgeable about how
Shakespearean verse works, it is unlikely to be less than an intense
emotional experience on even the most unsophisticated stage.

3

Cymbeline

Estrangement and Family Disruption

Without the play that bears his name, Cymbeline would be just
another semi-mythical English monarch known only to specialist
students of history. The connections between Shakespeare's king
and the historical accounts of him found in Holinshed's *Chronicles*
and elsewhere contain little that would suggest why Shakespeare
picked on him. Howard Felperin in his book *Shakespearean Romance*
(Princeton University Press, 1972) suggests Cymbeline's only significance was that he happened to be the English king at the time of
Christ's nativity, and he sees substantial evidence of Christian ethics
at work in the play's final scene. There is also the whole business of
Rome and the payment of tribute, which links *Cymbeline* with *King
Lear* as a play that takes place against a background of the threat
of invasion and loss of national identity. But an examination of
sources for the play is far more likely to highlight the romance
motif of the wager plot, which many critics locate most confidently
in Boccaccio's *Decameron*, than aspects of English history. Even were
we able to categorically identify, let alone understand Shakespeare's
attitude to his sources, we would not necessarily gain a firmer critical
grasp on the play itself. It is in many ways more fruitful to approach
the play knowing when it was written, confidently embracing it as a
late play.

The ruinous break-up of the family unit, in this case the English
royal household, takes place at a very early stage in *Cymbeline*. The rift

that occurs between the secretly married Posthumus and Imogen with Cymbeline in Act 1, Scene ii, is clearly the cause of far wider harm. A glance, literally, at the exchange between Imogen and Posthumus after the Queen has left them (1.ii.14–32) should suffice to reveal that there is something remarkably balanced about it, simply in terms of length. Imogen voices her sorrow and her husband responds with an equal measure of reassurance and comfort. But both speeches temper emotion with narrative information. Imogen opens by letting us know she has seen through the Queen's sympathy completely, and her choice of the word 'tyrant' introduces the wicked stepmother of fairy tale and romance. In fact Cymbeline's wife remains nameless throughout the entire play, emphasising her archetypal role. Posthumus, after expressing his own sorrow in feminine terms by asking her to stop crying in case she makes him weep too, assures her of his fidelity but then slips into humdrum practicality by describing in some detail where he will be living in order that she can write to him. Why is this dull matter given equal weight with the richer emotion? As in *Pericles*, it is the *nature* of Shakespeare's source that determines this. The wager plot that Shakespeare has possibly taken from Boccaccio's *Decameron*, the most well-known form of this tale, relies totally on the lovers communicating by letter. And although Shakespeare has watered down their effect substantially, letters still feature strongly in *Cymbeline*.

A look at the scant imagery used by the lovers to express emotion brings to light some useful information. Imogen finds her only comfort in the knowledge that 'there is this jewel in the world / That I may see again' (ll. 21–2). Posthumus is a paragon among men, something both rich and rare, an image entirely in keeping with the conflict she has with her father and her stepmother over their choice of husband for her, the corrupt, but regal, Cloten. A jewel, while materialistic, is nonetheless wholly fitting for the saintly Imogen, since she thinks only in terms of seeing her husband again rather than anything more sensual. Imogen's 'jewel' connotes constancy, durability and trust. If we compare this with Posthumus's imagery we find a stark contrast. Imogen is, firstly, both his 'queen' and 'mistress'. Though the former term implies loyalty, the latter is undoubtedly far more intimate – 'mistress' was conventionally used to describe the female object of a man's love and desire in love poetry of the period, although it did not foreground the illicit connotations it has today. He goes on to assure her he will be 'The loyal'st husband that did e're plight troth' (l. 27), yet Imogen has not even raised the issue of faithfulness. Loyalty, which in marriage hinges on fidelity, is clearly a vital concern to her husband, and his interest in sexual love is also hinted at in 'And with mine eyes I'll drink the words you send' (l. 31), which is as sensual as anything Romeo has to say. From the moment he opens his mouth, Posthumus is vulnerable.

When Shakespeare does allow some space for the lovers to continue their sorrowful parting, before Cymbeline and his entourage arrive, we find precisely the same determining factors controlling what is said. Posthumus expresses his 'loathness to depart' (ll. 37–9) wittily enough through the hyperbole proper to love poetry of the period, and then moves to go, which is clearly why he finishes with 'Adieu' in line 39. But he is dramatically stayed by Imogen's desire for some more fitting departure: 'Were you but riding forth to air yourself, / Such a parting were too petty. Look here, love' (ll. 41–2). With that, Imogen produces the diamond ring she wants him to wear. Considering her description of him, we may choose to see her giving him a 'jewel' as wholly appropriate. It is partly conventional, and demanded by the separation involved in the wager plot. What is far more intriguing is her suggestion that he wear it 'till you woo another wife, / When Imogen is dead' (ll. 43–4), which makes the ring nothing like a conventional love token. It begs a question. Why does Imogen talk of death and of Posthumus remarrying?

Just as Pericles, Thaisa and Marina appear dramatically insignificant amidst the fury of the storm, Imogen and Posthumus are flotsam in the unpredictable sea of Cymbeline's court. The opening speech of the play, as in *King Lear*, tells us that the state is a troubled one and the king unpredictable. Imogen knows that by rejecting the doltish Cloten, and by loving Posthumus, she has disturbed the balance of the entire court and rendered her own future uncertain. Her words surprise Posthumus, too, which we can see in his repeated questioning 'How, how? Another?' He vows faithfulness in an ominous image of death, putting on the ring with the ironic words, 'remain thou here, / ... While sense can keep it on' (1.ii.49). To counter her sad gesture of self-devaluation, Posthumus employs imagery of commerce to express how badly Imogen has done out of their marriage bargain in comparison to himself:

> As I my poor self did exchange for you
> To your so infinite loss; so in our trifles
> I still win of you.
>
> (1.ii.50–2)

A potent caesura then prepares us for his balancing gift. That they are balanced, that Shakespeare has designed and juxtaposed them for our benefit, is clear, yet what do we learn by comparing their two 'trifles'?

Imogen's gift of the ring comes with the selfless proviso that he wear it only while she lives, leaving him free to remarry should she die. Posthumus places a bracelet on her arm with the words,

> For my sake wear this,
> It is a manacle of love, I'll place it
> Upon this fairest prisoner.
>
> (1.ii.52–4)

However conventional a bracelet as a love token may be, Shakespeare makes it a 'manacle' and Imogen a 'prisoner' because the imagery prefigures Posthumus's sexual jealousy. Where Imogen is entirely innocent and generous in her gift, Posthumus is possessive and possibly even suspicious. Yet both 'trifles' are necessary features of the wager plot. What we see here is Shakespeare making dramatic sense out of intractable source material. His lovers have to be separated and Posthumus needs both a visible signal to initiate the discussion with Iachimo about his wife's virtue – the ring – and something similar to Desdemona's famous hankerchief with which Iachimo can taunt him later – the bracelet. In this parting Shakespeare neatly and efficiently provides both.

Brief though this parting is, Shakespeare has constructed it to make it absolutely credible so that Imogen's exclamatory 'O the gods! / When shall we see again?' (1.ii.55) may precipitate an embrace that would maximise Cymbeline's anger when he enters. But it is not merely Cymbeline's fury that prompts Posthumus to leave so abruptly with the briefest of final words for his wife and the king's entourage. It is simply unnecessary for Posthumus and Cymbeline to quarrel again. We know of their conflict, we know its cause and its false basis; what matters more is that Posthumus is seen to leave for Rome, and that Shakespeare makes him do it without delay. Yet if this is true, why then are we treated to a repeat of the quarrel between Imogen and Cymbeline?

Their argument, though fierce, is not sustained. It is a curt exchange in which each complaint is answered in its turn, rather than a single position developed by one of the parties. Once more, narrative concerns figure highly in this exchange, and information about Cymbeline, Imogen, Cloten and Posthumus, which has been related coldly to us by the First Gentleman in the play's opening scene, is here given flesh and blood.

The play opens with a description of Cymbeline's wrath and family discord. In scene ii, Shakespeare puts that disharmony on display for us but in as abbreviated a manner as possible within the strictures of effective dramatic presentation. There is a little more in the way of imagery here, but nonetheless, in comparison to what we may be used to in Shakespeare's earlier plays, this is still remarkably sketchy and underdeveloped. If we chose, for example, to concentrate wholly on Cymbeline's anger, and compare it with the wrath expressed by Lear when Cordelia fails his love test, we would find the former lacking in most respects. Nevertheless, the opening works in the same way to set up the disruption of the family that is central to the romance plot.

Flight and Foreigners

Both the lovers in Cymbeline are forced to flee for their lives, although while Posthumus has to deal directly with the culture of a foreign land and its inhabitants, Imogen's flight brings her into conflict with the natural world familiar to many exiles in Shakespeare's earlier plays.

A curious, but vital episode in *Cymbeline* occurs when we discover Posthumus safely in exile. It is vital because it initiates the wager plot upon which so much of the dramatic tension depends. What primarily makes this a curious passage is that it, and indeed the complete scene (1.v), is in prose. Prose in Shakespeare is usually reserved for lowly or rustic characters, such as the gaolers later on in *Cymbeline*. Interestingly, the only other character in the entire play who speaks in prose, and does so with absolute consistency, is the Queen's loutish son Cloten. Yet here, a small group of noblemen, of differing nationalities, are seated in conversation and they all speak in prose for the entire scene. Some editors explain this away by suggesting the scene is not by Shakespeare, without providing much in the way of substantial evidence, which is of little help. Concentrating on indications as to how this might be given life on stage, we find Posthumus has been spoken about before he makes his entrance and Iachimo has already made it clear by his sneering responses to the approval of others that he is unlikely to find much in Posthumus to please him. Philario's role throughout is reasonably neutral and if we are puzzled by his ultimate failure to defend Posthumus against Iachimo's obvious spite, we should remember he was a friend of Posthumus's father and there is a generation gap here which can easily account for that. Philario is too old and too wise to allow himself to become deeply embroiled in the passionate claims of young men eager to prove themselves. When Posthumus enters, therefore, we are half expecting trouble.

Present also, according to the text, are a Dutchman and a Spaniard who are mute throughout the scene, whose nationality might conceivably have been indicated by costuming. One of the things the theatre companies seemed to have been quite ready to spend money on was striking costume, and there are one or two accounts of some surprising sums involved. In the *Decameron* version, all of those present at the wager are Italian, but in another possible source of the same story, a prose version called *Frederyke of Jennen*, they are all of differing nationalities. What matters for us is that in Shakespeare's *Cymbeline* they are different, and two of them are mute throughout.

Jacobean England was a vehemently Protestant country steeped in religious controversy, in a Europe dominated by the Catholic Church in Rome. It was also a Europe in which travel was an arduous and time-consuming business for either the rich diplomat, or the poor soldier, but for very few other citizens. One nation's knowledge of another was a confused and complex affair frequently expressed by warfare. In such a world, conversations, in plays, about France and Italy are rarely innocent travelogues. For the average Englishman in 1609, 'Italian' was simply synonymous with villainy. Interestingly the Italian Renaissance sculptor Benvenuto Cellini, writing in his autobiography between 1558 and 1566, never fails to use the word 'English' without adding some insult stamping them brutish louts (Benvenuto Cellini, *Autobiography*, Penguin, 1998, p. 17).

Shakespeare's company, formerly the Lord Chamberlain's Men with the Puritan Earl of Essex as their patron, became the King's Men with royal patronage in 1603, after both the death of Essex (executed by Elizabeth in 1602) and the death of the Queen herself a year later. The story of King Cymbeline, as Shakespeare may have found it in Holinshed's *Chronicles*, is a confused and uncertain tale but it does contain the essential conflict between England and Rome which Shakespeare used to patriotic effect in his *Cymbeline*. Elizabethan and Jacobean playwrights worked within an atmosphere of political and religious uncertainty where prison was a very real danger for those who displeased the authorities. Royal patronage helped Shakespeare's company to survive, especially against the enmity of the City of London, and there were very good political reasons in 1609 or thereabouts, why Shakespeare would have chosen a story about an English king who successfully stands up against the power of Rome. Guy Fawkes and his associates had failed to blow up King James and his parliament in November 1605, and since then the King had been liable to respond rashly and prohibitively against any kind of threat, and even issued an edict in 1608 completely banning plays in London when George Chapman's play *The Conspiracy and Tragedy of Charles Duke of Byron* offended the French ambassador.

So we cannot ignore the nationalism we find in *Cymbeline* or sidestep it as the work of some collaborator. The Frenchman who opens the conversation with Posthumus in Act 1, Scene v, is all politeness. He reminds Posthumus of their previous acquaintance, to which Posthumus replies with equal courtesy, allowing the Frenchman to continue this game of civil exchange by saying he was glad to have been of assistance in preventing a quarrel taking place over a

'slight' and 'trivial' matter (l. 40). The formal politeness of their
speech is evident from the frequency with which they use 'sir', and
it can be no accident the word is dropped once Iachimo speaks. (It is
not used again until Posthumus employs it to address Philario when
he attempts to divert the growing dispute later in the scene at line 98.)
Posthumus tries to excuse his former behaviour by saying he 'was
then a young traveller' more likely not to respond to things he heard
rather than agree on the basis of others' experience, a characteristic
entirely credible in a young man of ambition and moral substance.
Yet such is his feeling for Imogen that he cannot even now let the
'slight' go unchallenged. Once more his language is rigidly formal and
polite, something clearly audible in the parenthetic 'if I offend not to
say it is mended' (ll. 44–5). At this point Shakespeare springs the well-
baited trap by allowing the Frenchman to make a gently ironic
reproof. The argument was indeed not 'slight', he suggests, since
two capable opponents were ready to kill each other over it. That is
the chink Iachimo has been waiting for.

It is worth contemplating his superficially innocent question carefully: 'Can we with manners ask what was the difference?' (l. 50).
Iachimo has as yet not addressed Posthumus, the newcomer to the
group, at all, and in this question he seems not to do so, for it is the
Frenchman who answers on Posthumus's behalf. His opening
'Safely, I think,' combined with the break which follows it, is the
kind of expression you would use if checking to see if the other party
(Posthumus) agrees, before you begin, again emphasising his good
manners. Iachimo's ambiguous use of 'manners' is itself intriguing. It
is as though he is mocking the other two for their obvious politeness
while simultaneously avoiding the risk of outright rudeness. We
should remember that everything he says before Posthumus enters
implies he is going to dislike the newcomer.

The Frenchman then explains and produces an impressive list of
adjectives, which we apply by association to Imogen, culminating in
the vital 'attemptable' which means something like 'seduceable'.
Iachimo's response, 'That lady is not now living; or this gentleman's
opinion, by this, worn out' (ll. 60–1), is crucial. The issue here is
chiefly about tone. How assertive is Iachimo? How angry is Posthumus? How could a director of the play reconstruct this episode to

make convincing dramatic sense? It is precisely the kind of episode in the late plays which proves a formidable hurdle for critics and directors alike, the former scavenging source texts for explanations, the latter resorting to stock types and gestures. Nonetheless, gesture may in effect help us here. What exactly does Iachimo mean when he says, 'by this' in line 61? He may mean something like 'evidently' or 'by the fact that the argument was ultimately given up' but if we take into account Posthumus's words moments later, when we cannot deny, however heated this argument is, that it has hotted up, we may see something else happening. When Posthumus says, 'Being so far provok'd as I was in France' (l. 64), we know that in France he was provoked to fight. If Iachimo's 'by this' also involves a gesture towards his sword, the conventional invitation to a fight, then Posthumus's words, and his civilised restraint, make more dramatic sense.

In this reading, Posthumus's 'She holds her virtue still, and I my mind' becomes a clinical and determined riposte where 'mind' refers back to Posthumus's 'mended judgement' (l. 44) and therefore equally his decision not to fight. Not surprisingly, then, considering how hard he has worked to goad Posthumus, Iachimo resorts to an even more direct challenge, which is in effect a simple threat, 'You must not so far prefer her 'fore ours of Italy' (l. 63). That Posthumus is trying his best to remain calm and civilised against this fairly crude attempt to quarrel is also discernible in the way he asserts his unchanged faith in Imogen. 'I would abate her nothing,' he says, adding, 'though I profess myself her adorer, not her friend' (ll. 65–6). That distinction is one we have to fully understand and it is one where modern etymology may intervene. The word 'friend' could be used to refer to an illicit partner of either sex and what Posthumus is doing is subtly distinguishing between what the Italian might be thinking about when he uses the word 'lady', and what he means. Posthumus emphasises that he is not only Imogen's lover, but her inferior, something the Frenchman, and possibly the others present, would appreciate. Recalling that there are others present is a healthy reminder that while they may be mute, they are nonetheless participants in this event and react accordingly or else are entirely superfluous. What this is leading us to is a recognition that nationalism plays a vital role in this whole episode. It is, of course, no accident that

Iachimo is Italian, when later on Cymbeline is to directly challenge the power of Rome, and Posthumus is to be a crucial participant in the battle that defeats the Romans.

Having failed with one form of assault, Iachimo then turns to another by shifting the argument wholly to the question of feminine virtue. And is this at all surprising when Posthumus, by his distinction between 'friend' and 'mistress', has in effect questioned any Italian's understanding of either word? 'As fair, and as good', Iachimo says, as though disbelieving the two could go hand in hand, before denying such a woman exists in Britain and manipulating the conversation towards his ultimate aim, the wager, via Posthumus's diamond ring. It is easy to neglect the fine irony here. The ring is Imogen's gift. It embodies her, and so when Iachimo asserts 'I have not seen the most precious diamond that is, nor you the lady' (ll. 72–3) he is playing ironically into Posthumus's hands. It is easy to imagine Posthumus looking down at the ring or toying with it as he replies, full of love and fond remembrance for Imogen and therefore increasingly invulnerable to Iachimo's taunts, 'I prais'd her as I rated her: so do I my stone' (l. 74). It is similarly not difficult to imagine Posthumus laughing, or at least smiling, as he says 'More than the world enjoys' (l. 76) when asked how much his ring is worth, since only he knows. Ignorant of how intimately Imogen and the diamond are woven together in Posthumus's mind, Iachimo tries a very logical riposte, 'she's outpriz'd by a trifle' (l. 78) because, logically, Posthumus's valuation of the ring debases Imogen. Posthumus tells them all that Iachimo is mistaken because a diamond may be sold or given away. The richness of the irony is exploited even further since he realises privately, but with the audience, that this particular diamond is beyond value and therefore it is unlikely anyone could provide 'wealth enough for the purchase' or indeed 'merit for the gift' (l. 81). It also allows him the opportunity to apostrophise Imogen again, where he describes her as 'only the gift of the gods' (l. 82), to which the increasingly frustrated Iachimo can only sneer, 'Which the gods have given you?' (l. 83).

At this point, wholly in control of both his emotion and the conversation, Posthumus concludes the extract with a suitably humble and gracious recognition of his own limitations, 'Which by their graces I will keep' (l. 84), while raising in the audience's mind all the tragic dangers such a remark conventionally hints at. Posthumus has performed admirably, for an Englishman, in this carefully constructed piece of anti-Catholic propaganda, resisting provocation and outwitting his opponent at a game Iachimo only managed to prove himself inept at.

But this is only part of the wider picture. Iachimo's choice of weak spot, Imogen's sexual fidelity, is ultimately successful and he succeeds in goading Posthumus far enough to make the wager. The increased tension is evident in Philario's efforts to divert the two parties after Posthumus has openly insulted Iachimo with the charge, 'I do nothing doubt you have store of thieves' (ll. 93–4). What we can conclude is that Iachimo's villainy works on Posthumus's sense of patriotism as well as his personal weakness, which, we have already observed, is his sexual perception of Imogen.

New Identities

In *Cymbeline*, the heroine is forced to change her identity but in this case willingly complies, and disguise is a paramount consideration. In Act 3, scene iv, Pisanio, Posthumus's servant, advises Imogen on how to escape the court and the unwelcome attentions of the Queen's son Cloten. Even a cursory glance at Pisanio's speech (3.iv.142–53) reveals Shakespeare using enjambement to convey excitement and urgency. Pisanio is eager to assist Imogen, and has already formulated a plan to do so. However, there is some troublesome imagery.

Pisanio suggests Imogen will need a mind 'Dark, as your fortune is' (l. 146), which may initially seem straightforward: Imogen's husband has asked Pisanio to murder her because he thinks she has been unfaithful; she is being pursued by a loathsome suitor; her father has rejected her and she has an openly evil stepmother to contend with. Whose fortune could be darker? But Pisanio is also employing a secondary sense for 'Dark' that links it cleverly with 'disguise'. The disguise he is talking about seems to have little connection with a physical disguise, as yet, because he asks, 'if you could wear a mind', not a cloak or a doublet, which all come later. Pisanio's concern is initially about Imogen's willingness to follow through what he suggests. He appears to doubt her ability to adopt a disguise. If that surprises us we need only remember just how extraordinarily virtuous Imogen is, as are all the heroines of the late plays. It is not surprising, then, that Imogen replies,

> O, for such means,
> Though peril to my modesty, not death on't,
> I would adventure!
> (3.iv.152–4)

So good is she, that the idea of deceiving anyone, for any reason, is seen as essentially corrupt, and dressing as a boy threatens her modesty or virtue. But as long as what she does is virtuous, Pisanio's suggestion is a risk she is prepared to take. Imogen's austerity is strikingly different from the playful antics of Rosalind in *As You Like It* or Viola in *Twelfth Night*.

Darkness and light provide the focus of almost all the imagery in this debate and far from being a piece of tedious practicality most directors want to get out of the way as quickly as possible, this extract uses poetry in the way we might expect from the mature Shakespeare. The interplay of light and dark continues in the difficult image, 'you should tread a course / Pretty, and full of view' (ll. 148–9). To an Englishman of Shakespeare's day the word 'course' was as strongly linked to hunting as it was to any sense of journey or route, as dogs were commonly used (by both rich and poor) to run down (course) prey such as hare and deer. The pleasure in such a hunt was wholly in seeing the dogs, usually only two, in competition with each other and watching the graceful skill of both dogs and prey. To be unsighted in such a hunt is extremely frustrating for the spectators. Knowing this, the image 'Pretty, and full of view' becomes relatively straightforward.

Pisanio's final point is that his plan would allow Imogen to be near enough to Posthumus's house, if not to actually see him, to make his every move knowable through report. In keeping with the dominant imagery it is Posthumus's invisibility which is made the issue.

Pisanio's second attempt at persuasion begins with a promise of conciseness, 'Well then, here's the point' (l. 155), but it takes him another twelve lines to reach it, prompting Imogen to interrupt with 'Nay, be brief' (l. 168). The verse here is typical of the late plays in the way it is driven by the necessities of the romance source, risking realism and drama for narrative information. Imogen is to disguise herself as a boy; she is to attach herself to Lucius and to be found by her brothers Arviragus and Guiderius, and the audience needs adequate preparation for this.

Pisanio does in fact get to the point eventually. 'You must forget to be a woman', he says (l. 156), before developing the point in detail. He does not say: dress yourself up convincingly, or cut off your hair, or change your name; all very conventional pieces of advice in such situations. Instead he concentrates on the need for Imogen to behave like a boy. His first suggestion, 'change / Command into obedience' (ll. 156–7), might initially seem to us to be the wrong way around. Surely as a woman and wife she will need to change obedience into command? But Imogen is primarily a princess, and so what Pisanio chooses first is the most difficult thing for her to do: to lose her habit of command and adopt one of obedience to her new master, Lucius. Secondly, she will have to exchange the timidity and coyness, 'fear, and niceness' (l. 157) characteristic of all women, for the bravado and loud brashness of a youth. Shakespeare's choice of animal for this simile, 'As quarrelous as the weasel' (l. 161), is not at all problematic in spite of what many editors may say. Anyone familiar with English wildlife knows how bold and aggressive weasels are for their size.

The pace of Pisanio's speech remains urgent because he has not yet come to the end of his little plot. But what is perhaps most interesting is the nature of Pisanio's advice. If the romantic source material is controlling the verse, why does Pisanio place such importance on Imogen's behaviour and not on the details of her dress or movements? We might find a reason by reflecting for a moment on the comedies and the complex levels of irony disguise creates there. Imogen is being played by a man, or more likely a boy. The moment we perceive this as a stage effect, the exchanges between Pisanio and Imogen here take on a very different dramatic hue. There is now

something inescapably comic in the manner in which Imogen responds to this particular piece of advice:

> Nay, be brief:
> I see into thy end, and am almost
> A man already.
>
> (3.iv.167–8)

Simultaneously, Shakespeare is very cleverly reinforcing the dramatic
illusion and our willing suspension of disbelief. Hot on the heels of
the joke comes Pisanio's retort, 'First, make yourself but like one' (l.
169), where what he means very specifically, from his subsequent
reference to the clothing, is that Imogen must now dress like a man.
Such a complex manipulation of stage reality is common in the
mature comedies, but it is demonstrably present in the late plays too.

Imogen's response to Pisanio's counsel is equally rewarding if we
concentrate on its tone. Whatever degree of excitement and confidence Pisanio has voiced, it does not seem to have infected Imogen.
'Thou art all the comfort / The gods will diet me with' (ll. 181–2) is
hardly enthusiastic, and yet, like other heroines in the late plays, she
puts her faith in those gods. With a distinct degree of stoical resignation she adds,

> This attempt
> I am soldier to, and will abide it with
> A prince's courage.
>
> (3.iv.184–6)

The whole scene began with an exhausted Imogen facing death at
Pisanio's hands in a wild country spot, and in this context it is not at
all surprising that she exhibits a sad resignation rather than a vital
eagerness. Like other heroic figures in the late plays, Imogen trusts
'good time' (l. 184). For her, time is a kindly figure. Besides Pisanio, it
is all she has on her side. Unlike Marina in *Pericles*, Imogen does
not take on a new identity against her wishes; nonetheless, the
necessity to adopt a new identity is something she is hardly content
with.

Trials and Tests

The test Posthumus faces is a severe one, although it is his wife's
virtue which is in question, not his. Iachimo returns from his journey
to England having secreted himself in Imogen's bedchamber. Although, as a Machiavellian Italian, he is undoubtedly naturally
equipped to convince Posthumus that Imogen has been unfaithful,
the question of why Posthumus fails is still the most fertile one to
pursue.

A number of answers might initially be offered. Iachimo provides
a weight of convincing evidence; he is remarkably skilful in the way
he uses that evidence; Posthumus is simply gullible. From a realistic
viewpoint, Iachimo is frequently the object of critical attention that
compares him unfavourably with Iago in *Othello*, while Posthumus's
gullibility is equally scorned. Such views are neither especially informative nor especially apt.

If we start with the opening lines of Act 2, Scene iv, we see
Posthumus in mid-conversation with Philario concerning Imogen's
honour. Posthumus expresses absolute confidence in her before
moving the conversation on to politics. Within the wider framework
of British and Italian relations, then, we are guided to concentrate on
the individual relation between Posthumus and Iachimo. As has
already been stressed, it is misleading to see the conflict between
the two men outside of the national context Shakespeare so firmly
provides.

Philario marks Iachimo's arrival, but it is Posthumus who speaks
to him first and even that apparently innocent comment contains
useful material. He does not greet him, as Philario does immediately
after (l. 29), but instead he remarks upon the speed of Iachimo's
return. Compared with his earlier performance, there is no sign at all
of amity or even formal etiquette from Posthumus. Why? What keeps
Posthumus from the exchange of formalities we would expect from
Shakespearean noblemen? His subsequent comment makes all clear:

> I hope the briefness of your answer made
> The speediness of your return.
>
> (2.iv.30–1)

It is Imogen and her fidelity that preoccupies Posthumus, in spite of his discussion with Philario about Rome and Britain. The 'answer' he refers to is of course Imogen's imaginary rejection of Iachimo's advances, but is the interest Posthumus expresses that of a husband who trusts his wife entirely? Is it not rather the interest of a man anxiously doubtful, already suspicious and even jealous? From the start, Posthumus appears willing to be convinced. He does not even begin his test from a position of strength.

This is made clearer when he interrupts Iachimo's eager compliment, 'Your lady, / Is one the fairest that I have look'd upon –' (ll. 31–2), with a reminder of their bargain, beginning 'And therewithal the best' (l. 33) only to degenerate into an entirely negative image which reeks of jealous voyeurism:

> or let her beauty
> Look through a casement to allure false hearts,
> And be false with them.
>   (2.iv.33–5)

Iachimo chooses not to exploit this obvious weakness yet, but delivers letters to Posthumus, and it seems likely that Shakespeare intended there to be a conventional pause before 'All is well yet' (l. 39), indicative of Posthumus's perusing, if not reading, the letters, before he returns to the matter foremost in his mind, Imogen's sexual behaviour:

> Sparkles this stone as it was wont, or is't not
> Too dull for your good wearing?
>   (2.iv.40–1)

Even when trying to sound confident, Posthumus's words seep ambiguity. He asks whether the ring is still as attractive to Iachimo as it was before his journey, or has it now lost some of its lustre, but because the ring is so tightly bound to Imogen in his mind, he ends up implying that she too may now be 'dull' and therefore faithless. Iachimo seizes his opportunity and in carefully chosen, gentlemanly terms, makes it clear he has seduced Imogen and won the ring.

The brevity of Posthumus's response, 'The stone's too hard to come by' (l. 46), underlines his shock, but does not amount to a very strong denial and again is painfully ambivalent. Not only is the ring itself not so easily parted with, but surely Imogen's honour is not so easily besmirched. In his element, relishing the sight of Posthumus squirming, Iachimo is confident enough to play with his words, 'Not a whit, / Your lady being so easy' (ll. 46–7). The rhythm puts a pause after 'whit', and places a pointed weight on the antithesis of 'hard', Iachimo's gleeful 'easy'. That Posthumus is wounded by Iachimo's needle wit is clear because he replies, 'Make not, sir, / Your loss your sport' (ll. 47–8), for the first time using the formal address 'sir' with barbed politeness. But instead of trusting Imogen he resorts to a guarded threat,

> I hope you know that we
> Must not continue friends.
>
> (2.iv.48–9)

which Iachimo is quick to neutralise by reminding him of the details of their bargain. There is an undeniable logic in his reasoning here which runs so counter to the facts that we are left astounded by Iachimo's gall. Not only does he claim to have won both Imogen's 'honour' and the ring, but in doing so he has not wronged either Posthumus or Imogen since he performed 'both your wills' (l. 55). This is another calculated stab at Posthumus's jealous heart, which instantly reacts:

> If you can make't apparent
> That you have tasted her in bed, my hand
> And ring is yours.
>
> (2.iv.56–8)

The caesura after 'yours' puts appropriate gravity on the renewed, overt threat which follows as Posthumus warns Iachimo that if he cannot prove Imogen's guilt, they must fight and one or both must die. This is a duel where one of the participants, Iachimo, knows exactly what weapon to choose at any one moment, while his opponent fumbles uncertainly for anything that comes to hand.

We noted earlier that Iachimo did not employ the formally polite term 'sir' in spite of other gentlemen present using it repeatedly. Here it is noticeable that he uses it to begin both the speeches he makes to defend himself against Posthumus's threats, lines 49 and 61. Why? If we remind ourselves of the wider framework of national identity within which this personal conflict takes place, Iachimo's use of 'sir' is easily explained. He knows that it is the most effective way to remind Posthumus (and by implication any Englishman) that he is being held to his word. Ironically, Posthumus's strength, his honour, is also his weak spot. Iachimo promises not only to provide evidence, 'circumstances' (l. 61), and to swear, 'confirm with oath' (l. 64) the truth of his statement, but is so confident of his evidence he believes the oath will prove superfluous.

Posthumus has little option, as a gentleman, but to allow him to 'Proceed' to the moment when Iachimo produces the bracelet. There is a notable contrast between Iachimo's detailed descriptions and Posthumus's mostly brief, dismissive replies. We are urged to ask why Iachimo does not triumphantly hand over the bracelet straight away. Of course, he realises that a detailed description of Imogen's bedchamber is no proof whatsoever. If we look back at his behaviour when in Imogen's bedchamber we can see that he knows this even as he is gathering the evidence in his little note-book:

> Ah, but some natural notes about her body
> Above ten thousand meaner moveables
> Would testify, t'enrich mine inventory.
> (2.ii.28–30)

He also knows precisely *why* some intimate physical details of Imogen's would carry so much weight since as he removes the bracelet he says,

> 'Tis mine, and this will witness outwardly
> As strongly as the conscience does within,
> To th' madding of her lord.
> (2.ii.35–7)

Iachimo knows exactly what he is doing throughout. He doesn't produce the bracelet straight away because that would spoil the fun. He produces it at exactly the right moment, when he has stretched Posthumus to breaking point on the rack of his own jealousy. Iachimo's pleasure at witnessing Posthumus's discomfort is extreme. It is the whole reason he has embarked on this challenge – the ring is merely a pretext. What Shakespeare writes for us to enjoy is a superbly timed and controlled piece of torture, with the torturer greedily lapping up the victim's pain, in itself something of a daunting realisation.

A look at Iachimo's first piece of evidence, the tapestry in Imogen's bedchamber, reveals just how consciously he is toying with Posthumus's jealousy, how much he delights in 'th' madding of her lord'. His very first detail is not material at all but is calculated to ignite Posthumus's jealous imagination:

> (Where I confess I slept not, but profess
> Had that was well worth watching)
> (2.iv.67–8)

For a split second it appears that he gives hope to Posthumus, 'Where I confess I slept not', but that is instantly dashed by the sexual ambiguity which follows, where 'watching' not only means lying awake for, but also witnessing. The arrogantly Italianate Iachimo isn't satisfied with claiming he has had sex with Imogen, it has to be spectacularly good sex too. His choice of the tapestry as the second piece of evidence tightens the screw since it depicts Antony and Cleopatra, and Iachimo's use of 'her Roman' (l. 70) implies a direct parallel between Imogen and Cleopatra, himself and Antony. The description of the tapestry is covertly sexual, 'swell'd' (l. 71) 'press' (l. 72) 'strive' (l. 73), and Iachimo makes that connection overtly by suggesting it was wonderfully life-like, again goading Posthumus's jealous imagination. Posthumus is stung so severely that he interrupts, yet he maintains an outward confidence, dismissing this evidence as information easily come by.

Iachimo's second description, of the chimney-piece, gives another twist to the screw as this time the subject is 'Chast Dian, bathing'

(l. 82). Diana is both a huntress and a virgin goddess, and once more Iachimo claims the sculpture was so incredibly life-like, 'the cutter / Was as another Nature' (ll. 83–4), inviting us, and Posthumus, to see it with him. Courageously, Posthumus dismisses this, too, for the same reason, adding that the work is 'much spoke of' (l. 87). Undeterred, Iachimo adds his less provocative description of the ceiling, and the Cupids that support the grate as fire-dogs, although their 'winking' (l. 89) hints at the amorous activities that are supposedly going on across the chamber. Posthumus manages to scrape together a degree of common sense to defend himself against this onslaught of imagery, and laughingly tries to put an end to it with, 'This is her honour!' (l. 91). He even appears for a moment to be aware of Iachimo's ability to manipulate him, when he adds the parenthesis '(and praise / Be given to your remembrance)' (ll. 92–3), highlighting how unlikely it is someone would remember all this so clearly.

Although he succeeds in preventing Iachimo describing more, the damage has been done and his jealousy delivers him bound and gagged to the scaffold when Iachimo responds by producing the bracelet. Fully in control, aware of precisely what stage he has brought Posthumus to, Iachimo exposes the bracelet with a delighted rhetorical flourish:

> Then, if you can
>
> *[Showing the bracelet.*
> Be pale, I beg but leave to air this jewel: see!
>
> (2.iv.95–6)

Iachimo's dramatic gesture is reminiscent of Mark Antony's 'If you have tears, prepare to shed them now' from *Julius Caesar* (3.ii.170), where Antony, too, is in supreme control of those he is addressing. It is as though, totally confident of the effect, he is saying 'If you are capable of being pale, then be pale now.' Whether 'pale' means wan, or indifferent or unmoved (editors disagree), it is clear Iachimo is challenging Posthumus to retain his superficially calm defence against this new, damning piece of evidence.

Indeed, so confident is he, that he announces his victory and claims the ring as his prize. The niggling, unclear phrase, 'And now 'tis up again', allows us to speculate on the actions which accompany this powerful moment on stage. Does Iachimo hold the bracelet up for all the audience to see? The Globe was a large space and large gestures were very likely the norm. Or does he slide up his sleeve to reveal the bracelet at line 95 then slide it back at 97, teasing Posthumus with just enough of a view to recognise it but not enough to be sure? That would make Posthumus's next, shocked speech more naturally effective:

> Jove! –
> Once more let me behold it: is it that
> Which I left with her?
> (2.iv.98–100)

Whether he has the bracelet in his own hands or not, Posthumus must be able to see it clearly as Iachimo turns the rack of his jealous imagination once more, this time in the most overt way possible, recreating the scene for us all:

> She stripp'd it from her arm: I see her yet:
> Her pretty action did outsell her gift,
> And yet enrich'd it too.
> (2.iv.101–3)

In desperation Posthumus clutches at any hope he can, suggesting she gave it Iachimo to give to him, a hope Iachimo easily quashes by asking him whether or not she says this in her letter.

Posthumus's emotion finally seeps through the superficial calm and he relinquishes all trust in Imogen, 'O, no, no, no, 'tis true. Here, take this too' (l. 106), and his ring with it, before venting his agony, and giving Iachimo even more pleasure. It seems at this point that Iachimo has won a massive victory, but the test is not over yet. In Posthumus's mind, the ring embodies Imogen's love for him, and so sure is he of her infidelity, it becomes something fatal to his sight, 'a basilisk' (l. 107). Shakespeare now makes Posthumus take two further steps towards complete failure of this test:

> Let there be no honour
> Where there is beauty: truth, where semblance: love,
> Where there's another man.
>
>   (2.iv.108–10)

The formal structure here is that of a prayer, but the wicked things Posthumus prays for would outrage a Jacobean audience. Posthumus is a victim, like Othello and Leontes, of the cruel absurdities of irrational jealousy, but that does not render him guiltless. The action he takes, the belief he now formulates, are both unambiguously immoral. Having prayed for deceit, he now adds to the sin by condemning all women as incapable of virtue:

> The vows of women
> Of no more bondage be to where they are made
> Than they are to their virtues, which is nothing.
>   (2.iv.110–12)

Yet the complex irony is that, if the saintly Imogen were unfaithful, this is a conclusion we might also reasonably reach. In this way Shakespeare evokes sympathy for Posthumus, even as he makes him fail the test. The voice of rationality intervenes in the form of Philario, who makes essentially the same common-sense objection to Iachimo's assertion as Posthumus did before Iachimo's use of imagery had stretched him to breaking point.

Posthumus grabs at this lifeline quickly but in doing so hands Iachimo precisely the cue he was waiting for, 'Render me some corporal sign about her' (l. 119). It is also noticeable how simple and unconvincing is his language here compared with the prayer he has just uttered. Posthumus cannot even grip the lifeline when it is thrown to him since it takes only an oath by Iachimo, 'By Jupiter, I had it from her arm' (l. 121), to make him weaken again.

Posthumus's speech now begins to be broken and emotional. There is repetition, 'Hark you, he swears: by Jupiter he swears' (l. 122), ''Tis true, nay keep the ring, 'tis true' (l. 123), and incomplete sentences, 'they induc'd to steal it?' (l. 125), 'And by a stranger?' (l. 126), both indicative of excitement. His choice of words becomes intemperate, 'whore' (l. 128), 'hell' (l. 129), and he ends by damning both Imogen and Iachimo openly, 'and all the fiends of hell / Divide themselves between you!' (ll. 128–9).

Such is his emotion, Philario is again moved to intervene, urging him to be patient. Patience is indeed the only virtue Posthumus can call upon. It is all that Pericles, Marina and Thaisa could employ in their own struggles with inimical events. It is the only defence for Hermione, too, and Philario, in his insistence on it, 'Quite besides / The government of patience!' (ll. 149–50), is old enough and wise enough to know it is the only defence also, for Posthumus.

But Posthumus's jealousy makes him wallow in his own discomfort, and he feeds it with lascivious images of his own, 'She hath been colted by him' (l. 133), succumbing absolutely to Iachimo's torture. As we learned from his words in Imogen's bedroom, Iachimo's pleasure is more to drive Posthumus distracted than to take his ring from him. There is no need for him to describe the mole beneath Imogen's breast beyond the desire he has to see his victim writhe in agony. He is therefore extremely careful to maximise the potency of his little story. With clinical precision he describes the whereabouts of the mole – under Imogen's breast – since that would make it impossible for it to be seen under any but amorous circumstances. The rhythm places timely stress on the 'under' of line 134, and a caesura in line 136 prepares Posthumus for the maddening image of Iachimo kissing the mole. As a further insult, Iachimo once more claims that Imogen was a more than eager participant, 'and it gave me present hunger / To feed again, though full' (ll. 137–8). With all the skill of a professional, Iachimo adds the kind of twist which Shakespeare's audience may well have considered as both Italian and youthful arrogance. He hints at the idea that perhaps Posthumus may never have been so intimate with Imogen as to have seen the mole, 'You do remember / This stain upon her?' (ll. 138–9).

Such is the pleasure Iachimo gains in torturing Posthumus, that he is even capable of overstretching himself, 'Will you hear more?' (l. 141). Of course he has no further evidence, but is perfectly ready to indulge in some more, we can guess, highly imaginative descriptions of sex with Imogen. Posthumus appears to know that is what Iachimo means:

Spare your arithmetic, never count the turns:
Once, and a million!

(2.iv.142–3)

Once is as bad as a million times and Iachimo cannot make Posthumus more unhappy than he now is. Yet even now, Iachimo's greed
for pain drives him to attempt another turn of the rack and in his
agony Posthumus interrupts his 'I'll be sworn –' (l. 143) before he can
poison his mind with another haunting image of his unfaithful wife.

Like a wild animal at the stake, Posthumus's anger now erupts as
he threatens to kill Iachimo if he denies one word of what he has
said. He turns on Imogen in a fury of frustration and pain, 'O, that I
had her here, to tear her limb-meal!' (l. 147), then tries to employ his
jealous imagination as a weapon, only to leave the stage in a frenzied
state of impotence:

I will go there and do't, i' th' court, before
Her father. I'll do something –

(2.iv.148–9)

It is left for Philario to formally declare Iachimo's victory, and to
follow Posthumus to prevent him harming himself, such is the level
of his distress. Quite what a Jacobean audience, absolutely in tune
with the nationalism that, we have argued, frames the entire wager
sub-plot, would have made of Iachimo's 'With all my heart' (l. 151), is
difficult to conjecture, but its effect seems to be to confirm Iachimo
as a type of Italianate villain who enjoys creating grief and suffering.

Time and Tide

The movement between court and country – the juxtapositioning of
order and nature – figures prominently in Shakespeare's comedies
and occurs again in the late plays. Pericles is thrown ashore on a wild
beach to be rescued by simple fishermen. Florizel and Perdita in *The
Winter's Tale* inhabit a pastoral Arcadia before the reality of the court
catches up with them, and in *Cymbeline* the audience is abruptly taken

to the wilds of Wales early in Act 3, where they are introduced to the renegade Belarius and his nominal sons, Cadwal (Arviragus) and Polydore (Guiderius).

Time is apparently an enemy to Arviragus and Guiderius. Regaled with stories of their father's past life and glories, they can only feel frustrated and envious. Arviragus imagines future winter evenings in their crude cave empty of 'discourse' since they have lived lives wholly free from contact with the larger world. Their 'valour' (3.iii.42) he dismisses as 'beastly' (l. 40), and he likens them to caged birds that sing to soften the pain of their imprisonment. However wild his appearance, his words are anything but coarse. Shakespeare's audience would have been quick to read the signals in his verse that imply he is noble. His use of rhetorical questions, his desire for civilised 'discourse', the witty paradox, 'Our valour is to chase what flies' (l. 42), combine to stamp him with nobility. We have only to think of the words Shakespeare puts into the mouths of his undisguised rural characters, the shepherd and clown in *The Winter's Tale* for example, and the point becomes obvious. In view of this, Belarius's reprimand, 'How you speak!' (l. 44), may even be a sophisticated joke.

Belarius's diatribe to his impatient sons (3.iii.45–64) is easily divisible. The first half concentrates on the dangers of the court and warfare. The second places Belarius firmly in the Cymbeline story as a loyal general poorly treated, via his conceit of the fruit tree, one day laden with fruit, and the next blasted and stripped bare. Belarius's sententious commentary is a fine contrast to Polonius's infamous advice to Laertes in *Hamlet* and provides us with sharp insights into the reality of Jacobean society. He demonises the city, 'Did you but know the city's usuries' (l. 45), but shows great wisdom in his subtle addition, 'And felt them knowingly'. It is not enough to be warned, one has to feel the dangers too. The art of being a successful courtier he sees not only as something intrinsically paradoxical, 'As hard to leave as keep' (l. 47), but as something doomed to ultimate failure since whoever succeeds in climbing the heights of courtly power is certain to fall. Yet this is not all. Belarius adds to the image of climbing, the subtle idea that the route is so 'slipp'ry', the fear which grips you is as bad as the fall itself. It is an enticingly credible picture of any European Renaissance court. Paradox permeates the art of warfare too. The 'pain' or effort of seeking glory vanishes even as it is gained. When victory is gained, the victor is as likely to be slandered by history as to be honestly reported, and often his good actions lead to bad ends. Belarius crowns this catalogue of evil with the ultimate insult to the honourable man. Admonished for his failure, he must nonetheless smile at his own humiliation, 'Must court'sy at the censure' (l. 55). Belarius invites his sons to trust him since he is living proof of all this.

Belarius's downfall is similar to Prospero's, and like Prospero's, it involves banishment from the court to the wilderness. Whereas Prospero's salvation is magic, Belarius's is nature, the joy that he derives from the hunt and the daily struggle to survive, which, like Prospero's magic, brings as consolation, a closeness to God. As though aware of his own self-indulgence, Belarius breaks off and turns his attention back to the hunt, yet so intrinsically woven into his life is the pain of his banishment, he cannot maintain any conversation for long without returning to it. No sooner has he urged his sons on with promise of reward,

> he that strikes
> The venison first shall be the lord o' th' feast,
>
> (3.iii.74–5)

than he reminds them of the evil they have escaped at court:

> And we will fear no poison, which attends
> In place of greater state.
>
> (3.iii.77–8)

Time is undoubtedly a great healer in these plays, but forgetfulness is never a part of that healing process, as Prospero, Pericles, Leontes and Belarius so powerfully demonstrate. Time permits a greater understanding of the processes that have led the individual to a given crisis. It doesn't erase that crisis or its long-term effects.

With his sons out of the way hunting, Belarius is free to pass on the narrative information which the audience has been half expecting since the loss of the brothers was first made significant at the very start of the play. 'How hard it is to hide the sparks of Nature!' (l. 79) Belarius exclaims, adding that though brought up in a cave, the boys strive for 'The roofs of palaces' (l. 84). Even in the simplest of actions, their princely natures are revealed. Polydore, the eldest and heir to the throne, is so imaginatively gripped by Belarius's tales of war, he re-enacts them. Cadwal, the younger, does so too but with a greater imagination of his own, as though the second son were conventionally more creative. In the world of these plays, and in many of the comedies, blood kinship is an irrefutably positive force. The weight of scholarship over the centuries has dwelt on exploring monarchy as possibly the central aspect of Elizabethan and Jacobean culture, as well as of a larger metaphysical framework. Yet certainly in the late plays, the king is also just as significantly a father and a husband. The idea of the natural family, where children are the products of loving relationships, has at least an equal claim on our critical attention. In calling our attention to the impossibility of disguising the princes' royal nature, Belarius is reminding the audience of their own essentially human ties and responsibilities while suggesting that, in some ways, time cannot destroy people's innate nature.

Suffering and Forgiveness

The suffering Posthumus undergoes in *Cymbeline* is not to be compared to that of Pericles, either in terms of time or in degree, yet the suffering he does endure is sufficient to push him to the very brink of life. Captured and manacled on the battlefield, convinced his wife has betrayed him, he spends a night alone, in the open and the dark, yet hobbled to the earth, contemplating his appalling fate. Posthumus's thoughts are almost bafflingly paradoxical. His whole situation strangely amuses, yet appals him, and he begins his reflections by noting the paradox:

> Most welcome bondage; for thou art a way
> I think to liberty.
>
> (5.iv.3–4)

The depth of suffering he has reached then becomes clear as he openly uses another paradox in which Death is made the means to alleviate his pain. After he jokes darkly about his current captivity, a caesura marks his shift of thought from the captivity of his body, to the captivity of his eternal soul, and deftly, Shakespeare maintains the prison imagery to link the two ideas:

> My conscience, thou art fetter'd
> More than my shanks and wrists: you good gods, give me
> The penitent instrument to pick that bolt,
> Then free forever.
>
> (5.iv.8–11)

The density of this image is exemplified by the ambiguity surrounding 'The penitent instrument', which on one level is clearly Death, but also appears to refer to Posthumus's desperate need for absolution. Penance is a means of atoning for one's sins, a means to cure a sick soul and guilty conscience, and make it whole again. What Shakespeare is doing in this scene is showing us Posthumus actually going through the process of understanding his guilt and seeking a means to atone for it. That process is driven by a kind of crystalline reasoning, and there is something very reminiscent of Hamlet in the way Posthumus climbs the steps of his own rationality. 'Is't enough I am sorry?' (l. 11) he asks himself, and again a caesura isolates this question for special consideration. 'So children temporal fathers do appease,' he answers, dismissing the idea that his guilt might be as insignificant as a child's, while acknowledging that 'Gods are more full of mercy' (l. 13). A second question: 'Must I repent?' is answered by Posthumus admitting his current state of captivity is welcome, suggesting therefore that it is the ideal opportunity for repentance. Posthumus employs a theological vocabulary, 'sorry', 'repent' and 'satisfy', which specifically defines the three stages that any soul must experience before it can receive remission for its sins. Throughout, his speech is as much with God as with himself, and his request to God to 'take / No stricter render of me than my all' (ll. 16–17) forms the culmination of his sophisticated reasoning.

As though he feels unanswered, Posthumus resumes his prayer, seeking hope in God's clemency. He describes the way 'vile men' will take only a portion of the debts they are owed in hope to gain more from prolonging the suffering of their debtors. God, he knows, is 'more clement' and so he states, 'that's not my desire', before confirming lucidly the bargain he wishes to make, 'For Imogen's dear life take mine' (l. 22).

Suffering in these plays also generates humility, and Posthumus admits that, although compared with Imogen's, his life is 'not so dear', yet he is no less a child of God, ''tis a life; you coin'd it' (l. 23). Toying with the notion that coins bear the image or 'stamp' of the king, Posthumus suggests that the stamp alone is enough to give the coin value and not every coin is weighed meticulously. His own coin, 'Though light' (l. 25), he asks God to take 'for the figure's sake', since it is God's image. Once more it is through paradox that Posthumus reaches understanding. Posthumus has, in effect, reasoned his own soul into a state of harmony with his God and maker, and so there is no more questioning in the final appeal, only resignation. The 'audit' Posthumus regards as the process of reasoning to which he has just submitted his own soul. Knowing he is entirely in God's hands, he sleeps, the wish that in eternal life he will meet Imogen again, forming a paradoxical prayer on his exhausted lips:

> O Imogen,
> I'll speak to thee in silence.
> (5.iv.28–9)

In his handling of Posthumus and his change of heart, Shakespeare is often criticised, but he has expended considerable effort not only in depicting Posthumus's suffering, but in delineating the relationship between suffering, forgiveness and ultimately redemption. To look for reasons why Posthumus has decided he was wrong about Imogen is in one crucial sense to miss the point of forgiveness entirely. It was never Posthumus's right or role to punish her, whatever she did, and so in this scene, under the open skies and scrutiny of the heavens, Posthumus is free to experience the reality of guilt and the process of true penitence that leads him to wish to pay the ultimate price. In spite of the curious nature of divinity in these plays and *Cymbeline* especially, what Posthumus does is strive for a very Christian ideal: 'greater love hath no man than this, that a man lay down his life for his friends' (St John 15:13).

Divine Magic

Shakespeare's use of classical mythology in the late plays is entirely conventional and all he expects of his audience is that they know the basic functions of the gods he chooses, whether Greek or Roman. For example, it is Juno, Ceres and Iris who bless the union of Ferdinand and Miranda. Juno, as the Roman equivalent of Hera, the chief female divinity, represents all women and childbirth; Ceres is the Roman goddess of grain and agriculture, while Iris is the Greek goddess of the rainbow. It is tempting to think, especially in the period when the court masque was gaining popularity, that his choice of someone like Iris may have been dictated as much by purely visual potential as by her divine role.

In Act 5, Scene iv, the ghosts of the Leonati visit the sleeping Posthumus, and are reprimanded by Jupiter. This theophany has been the subject of considerable critical debate about authenticity. Jupiter's descent on a eagle is unusual, since simple thrones were the normal transport used to convey the gods, but a growing taste for ornamentation on stage, combined with the move to indoor theatres like that at Blackfriars, was unlikely to have passed Shakespeare by and certainly not younger writers, like John Fletcher, with whom he collaborated in his last plays and who replaced him as the chief writer for the company. Jupiter's hurling a thunderbolt is equally intriguing, and must have been an opportunity for a technical spectacle of some kind. It is almost certain that music would also have played a significant role in this whole scene. But in the absence of the sort of evidence we would need to recreate these elements, the poetry has to be our most trustworthy guide.

Jupiter's verse uses alternate rhyme. In his angry rebuke of the Leonati, although there is sufficient enjambement to avoid the stulti-fying dullness that would result without it, the alternate rhyme still thumps through the entire speech sufficiently to be heard, while a striking rhyming couplet concludes it. The question we should ask is, why is Jupiter's speech given a form of its own? The moment he departs, the Leonati speak in blank verse again (even though their own verse form earlier in the scene was itself distinctly not iambic pentameter). We have already seen in *Pericles* that Shakespeare gave Gower a distinct verse form of his own in keeping with his role as an ancient poet, 'From ashes ancient Gower is come' (1. chorus. 2), and in *Hamlet*, the visiting players demonstrate their art in verse that is wholly different from the blank verse that surrounds it. The 21 lines of poetry given to Jupiter are enough to distinguish him from the ghosts and the mortals in this scene.

He refers to the ghosts of Posthumus's family as 'petty spirits of region low' (l. 93) and silences them with imperatives, 'No more,' and 'hush!' before urging them back to 'Elysium'. Then his annoyance appears to dissipate in the pity of 'Poor shadows' and the comforting image of the 'never-withering banks of flowers' (l. 98), and he even gives them a reason for his rebuke, reminding them that earthly events are no concern of theirs, but his.

His original, dramatic, irate appearance is superseded by a benevolent, calm reassurance which ends in:

> Whom best I love, I cross; to make my gift,
> The more delay'd, delighted.
>
> (5.iv.101–2)

It is risky to argue on aesthetic grounds that this compact, witty expression is unlikely to be Shakespeare's. Not only is there the witty conjunction of 'delay'd' and 'delighted', but there is the powerful paradox of his hurting those he loves most, which becomes doubly paradoxical if we see an implied blessing behind the words 'cross'. A contemporary audience would be unable to hear the word without its Christian connotation, or the gesture of blessing it signifies. There is even the possibility that 'best' is intended to echo 'blest'. In *Much Ado About Nothing*, the envious Don John says of Claudio, 'If I can cross him any way, I bless myself every way' (*Much Ado About Nothing*, 1.iii.70), making the link between 'cross' and the gesture of blessing clear.

Yet it is the idea itself that is most significant, rather than the witty verse which expresses it. In it lies the key to the suffering of a long list of characters in the late plays, from Pericles to Prospero.

It contains the dramatic principle that underpins all of the late plays. The dramatic impact Shakespeare generates in the climax of these somewhat awkward plays relies heavily on the skilful manipulation of three fundamental elements: suffering, delay and restitution. The greater and more unjust the suffering, and the longer the delay, the greater the audience's delight at the final restoration. Which is why *Pericles* is the most moving of the late plays, with *The Winter's Tale* a close second.

Jupiter's conciliatory tone continues as he tells the ghosts, 'Be content' (5.iv.102), since whatever depths of despair Posthumus has plumbed will be more than balanced by his generosity. This key principle, of reward for suffering, is repeated in 'His comforts thrive, his trials well are spent' (l. 104), as well as 'And happier much by his affliction made' (l. 108). He reminds them of his personal interest in Posthumus's fate, before predicting his restoration to Imogen, which prepares us not only for Posthumus's ultimate 'delight', but for Imogen's too.

Instructing the ghosts to place the tablet detailing Posthumus's fate on his chest, Jupiter dismisses them imperiously and departs himself in whatever visual splendour the technicians of the day could conjure up. The dialogue between the ghosts which covers his departure (ll. 114–22), presumably out of sight into the upper space of the theatre, is intriguing because of the faint glimpse it allows us into the theatre practice of the time. We are used to Shakespeare's characters, in the absence of lighting or effects, using poetry to engage our imaginations and creating the scene for us, whether simply to announce the dawn, or to detail the complex action of an offstage battle. In this curious episode from *Cymbeline*, we appear to have the same thing occurring, yet simultaneously the action involves about as complex and sophisticated a piece of stage mechanics as exists in the entire Shakespeare canon. The simple question we are left with is this. If an actor playing Jupiter was lowered to the stage inside, or mounted on, a piece of stage machinery painted to look like his divine eagle, why do the ghosts need to describe him doing so?

The first part of Sicilius's speech is in the past tense and could be seen merely as an expression of wonder (although ghostly wonder is itself perhaps a little problematic), if it were not that the second half of his speech (ll. 116–18) uses the present tense:

> He came in thunder; his celestial breath
> Was sulphurous to smell: the holy eagle
> Stoop'd, as to foot us.
>
> (5.iv.114–16)

With its emphasis on the senses, this seems to be precisely the kind of poetry we are used to when the technical limitations of Shakespeare's theatre require him to engage our imaginations. But it shifts, even within a single line, into something more problematic.

> His ascension is
> More sweet than our blest fields; his royal bird
> Prunes the immortal wing, and cloys his beak,
> As when his god is pleased.
>
> (5.iv.116–18)

That Sicilius is describing Jupiter's ascent in real time becomes even more likely when he makes his departing speech, 'The marble pavement closes, he is enter'd / His radiant roof' (ll. 120–1). This sounds very much as though a trapdoor in the roof of the theatre has closed to re-admit the eagle and its divine cargo, something that in either an indoor theatre, or the Globe, the audience could probably see for itself.

A clue to this tantalising problem may lie in the image Sicilius uses to describe the eagle's flight to earth, 'the holy eagle / Stoop'd, as to foot us', he says. To a Jacobean audience, even a London or courtly one, the language of hunting and in this case, falconry, presents no problem at all. They would know that the verb used to describe the spectacular, high-speed dive of any hawk as it attacks its prey, is 'to stoop'. It is an action in harmony with the other grandiose images surrounding Jupiter's appearance. It is also an action impossible to imagine even the sophisticated stage machinery of the present time mimicking successfully. What is more likely is that the machine which took the actor playing Jupiter up and down was so obviously crude and absent of any attempt at verisimilitude, either of appearance or of movement, that Shakespeare felt the need to employ his usual tactic, poetry, to compensate.

Jupiter and the ghosts gone, Posthumus awakes and the magical nature of the events comes to the fore. He makes it clear that he, too, has been privy to the vision we have seen, and his sorrow at finding the ghosts of his family gone melts indistinguishably into the realisation that he is awake. Initially, it seems as though his suicidal frame of mind has stayed with him. But he finds renewed hope merely in finding himself still alive, as Jupiter predicted:

> But, alas, I swerve:
> Many dream not to find, neither deserve,
> And yet are steep'd in favours; so am I
> That have this golden chance and know not why.
> (5.iv.129–32)

When he notices the tablet Jupiter instructed the ghosts to place on his chest, Posthumus immediately assumes magic to be the cause: 'What fairies haunt this ground?'

The prediction (ll. 138–44) is a simple allegory, although ironically too difficult for Posthumus to fathom. The audience recognises him as the 'lion's whelp', Imogen as the 'piece of tender air', Cymbeline as the 'stately cedar' and the lost sons Arviragus and Guiderius, the 'lopp'd branches'. It promises joyful restoration, the 'delight' of all the late plays, but Posthumus expresses bafflement in lines that have frustrated editors because their meaning is so condensed. Posthumus thinks he may still be dreaming, since the meaning of the book eludes him, or else it is that the prose is itself mere madness, like a madman speaking recognisable words, but without meaning. To emphasise his frustration he adds that it is 'either both, or nothing', because he has found it under such strange, magical circumstances that it ought to contain meaning and to dismiss it as 'nothing' denies the reality of its discovery. Confident that he is dealing with magic, Posthumus chooses the image 'speaking' for a particular reason, because he recognises what he has read as a riddle, and of course riddles promise truth. The prose should 'speak' to him, should make sense, but doesn't. It is either 'senseless' or makes a sense which he cannot fathom. His final words now knit very comfortably into the preceding density:

> Be what it is,
> The action of my life is like it, which
> I'll keep, if but for sympathy.
>   (5.iv.149–51)

Posthumus has understood enough of what has happened to him in the past hours to impute a magical and personal significance to the book, and under such circumstances it would be folly to ignore it, so he keeps it.

Revived Families

At the end of *Cymbeline* (in the words of a modern-day English playwright), 'the sky is black with chickens coming home to roost'. It isn't surprising that both Dr Johnson and George Bernard Shaw wrote scathingly of the play because of what they perceived as the absurdities in its concluding scene. So many loose ends are firmly knotted that there isn't space in this study to examine the restoration of Cymbeline's entire family. Instead, we will concentrate on the reconciliation of Cymbeline with his sons Guiderius and Arviragus, Imogen having already been rediscovered in the guise of Fidele.

Having explained how he slew Cloten, Guiderius is instantly condemned by Cymbeline. The war with Rome over, his army victorious, Cymbeline's power has been fully restored and his present business before the court is openly concerned with reward and punishment, the administration of justice. This provides Belarius with the motive to begin his revelations, and in the manner in which he addresses Cymbeline, we can discern a clear confidence and perhaps a hint of personal revenge. He issues the king with an imperative, 'Stay, sir king' (5.v.301), and reveals a similar disregard for the office of state by

ordering the king's guard to loose his hold on Guiderius, 'Let
his arms alone, / They were not born for bondage' (ll. 305–6).
Even more marked is the hyperbole of his riddling praise for
Guiderius.

Cymbeline clearly regards Belarius's words as treacherous and is
not beyond a little irony himself when he reminds Belarius that he is
as yet 'unpaid' for his performance in the battle, but he is intrigued
enough to question Guiderius's descent. Belarius continues to sound
enigmatic when he is unimpressed by Cymbeline's threats:

> We will die all three,
> But I will prove that two on's are as good
> As I have given out him.
>
> (5.v.310–12)

Is Belarius suggesting that they will all die if he doesn't prove what he
has said about Guiderius's descent? Or is he speaking with more
authority, and merely asserting the truth of what he is about to
reveal? In which case, 'But' is synonymous with 'nonetheless'. The
sons are quick to defend their father. Their combined words are
fiercely loyal and forthright. 'Your danger's ours' (l. 314) Guiderius
replies, 'And our good his' (l. 315), adds his brother, which becomes
virtually a threat via its assertion that they are all three inseparable.
What they demonstrate is a family unity strong enough to defy the
king. That is why Belarius employs such a belligerent opening to his
defence. He even appears to be aware of how far they have strayed in
that direction because he immediately qualifies his challenge with, 'by
leave' (l. 315). Belarius's earlier statement, 'We will die all three', now
becomes yet another arrogant rebuke in which he simply acknowledges that death will indeed come to all three of them, eventually.

This interpretation grows even more convincing if we recall that all
of this is taking place in the immediate aftermath of a bloody and
fierce battle in which Belarius and his sons, together with Posthumus,
have virtually won the day. Belarius, Guiderius and Arviragus share
with Posthumus a brutish strength and savagery, theirs derived from
their wild life, his from despair. Iachimo has earlier been seen almost
dying from his wounds – and add to this the blow from Posthumus

which fells Imogen, and there is considerable interest in physical demeanour and activity in this scene. So there is something entirely appropriate for the audience in this shocking confrontation with the ancient, gullible Cymbeline. In addition, to evoke a confrontational tone immediately prior to the recognition, heightens the dramatic effect through contrast. The wider the gulf to be bridged, the greater the impact of success.

Having revealed his own identity, Belarius confronts Cymbeline's renewed attempt at condemnation with vigorous confidence and irony, 'Not too hot; / First pay me for the nursing of thy sons' (ll. 322–3). The condition he attaches, that the money be confiscated as soon as he receives it, keeps up the conventional, riddling tone. Cymbeline's incomplete question, 'Nursing of my sons?' (l. 325), suggests both incomprehension and surprise. But Belarius cannot maintain his arrogant tone for long, his loyalty and sense of duty prevail, conveyed perhaps more powerfully by the gesture than the words, 'I am too blunt, and saucy: here's my knee' (l. 326). The treatment here of themes of loyalty, respect and age are clearly reminiscent of *King Lear*, and Belarius may owe a great deal to the irascible, disguised Kent.

On his knees, Belarius begins a lengthy exposition of the history of the two boys, directing everything in this part of the scene towards Cymbeline. *He* is the focus of the 'delight' and not his sons, or Imogen. This is possibly difficult to appreciate since he has been largely peripheral as a character, remarkably so if we compare him, for example, with Lear, or more pertinently here, with Pericles, Leontes or Prospero. Shakespeare gives neither Arviragus or Guiderius a word to express their feelings on discovering their true father; even Imogen is allowed only a very simple expression of joy and a moment to embrace them, and then as much because she has been reunited with Polydore and Cadwal as with her natural brothers.

Undoubtedly, Cymbeline is the centre of this entire reconciliation, and this is one of the reasons why, in performance, it falls far short of the emotion or beauty nascent in *Pericles* or *The Winter's Tale*. In the former, Marina's gradual awakening to the truth is made to perform an intricate ballet with Pericles' own, and in the latter, justice for Hermione is as significant a force as restoration is for Leontes and

Perdita. The audience's emotional investment is far higher in both these plays than in *Cymbeline*. There is not space to investigate it here, but considering whose 'delight' carries the audience's hopes most strongly along with it, is an interesting question to apply to the entire final act of *Cymbeline*.

Belarius reinforces the loyalty, dramatically asserted by his posture, as he denies fathering the boys and tells Cymbeline 'They are the issue of your loins' (l. 331), adding in a biblical tone, 'And blood of your begetting' (l. 332). Cymbeline's shocked questions prompt Belarius to embark on a detailed account of their abduction. Apart from the conventional practice of filling in the biographical gaps, it is significant that Belarius stresses their noble upbringing. Just as Marina is the nonpareil in her world of music and tapestry, Cymbeline's sons are equally above the common run of mankind. This resemblance is one of those aspects of the late plays that reveals how deeply linked romance always is with fairy tale.

One further aspect of Belarius's confession worth dwelling on is the honesty with which he imparts the truth of his own motivation and behaviour. Not only does he free Euriphile, their nurse, from all blame, but he openly acknowledges revenge as his own motive. He is not afraid to name his crime 'treason', nor to admit the pleasure he gained in the act, and in the first words Cymbeline uses in response we find an important clue to performance. 'Thou weep'st' (l. 353) Cymbeline says, and it must be that in this public announcement, Belarius has found a private relief. His use of 'benediction', 'heaven' and 'heavens', all in the last three lines of his confession, reveal a distinctly metaphysical frame of mind.

Significantly, in view of what we have already noted about the limited emotional impact of this recognition scene compared with *Pericles* or *The Winter's Tale*, Cymbeline now suggests that the service performed in battle by the three is more incredible than the story of their abduction. At the very moment of recognition, Cymbeline's interest seems to be as much in issues of blood and nobility as in paternal joy. In examining Iachimo's torturing of Posthumus, we noted how there was undoubtedly a concern with national identity in *Cymbeline*. Similarly there is a tension at the end of this play between the emotional demands of familial recognition, and the patriotic demands of nationalism. Yes Cymbeline's family is reunited, but the nation too has been restored, and perhaps the latter eventuality claimed as much of the Jacobean audience's dramatic sympathy as the former does today. This tension is equally discernible in Cymbeline's acceptance of the truth. His rhetorical questions,

> O, what am I?
> A mother to the birth of three?
> (5.v.369–70)

ring strangely hollow if set against the resounding words and tears of Pericles, or Leontes' awed kiss. In spite of his assertion, 'Ne're mother / Rejoic'd deliverance more' (ll. 370–1), he moves immediately to matters of state. His emphasis on their royal blood and rightful inheritance even leads him to turn to Imogen and remind her that she is, by her brothers' restoration, disinherited. But Imogen toys wittily with Cymbeline's astronomical image, 'No my lord; / I have got two worlds by 't' (ll. 374–5), suggesting generously that she has the better deal.

In comparison with her father, Imogen speaks with a sisterly joy untainted by notions of state. She calls them 'gentle brothers' and reminds them that it was she who called them brothers as Fidele, little knowing how prophetic her instinct was. Her speech is excitedly broken, and there is something undeniably amusing in her competitive claim, 'O, never say hereafter / But I am truest speaker' (ll. 376–7). Cymbeline can only utter a baffled half-line, 'Did you e'er meet?' (l. 379), and his two sons are given the most peremptory words themselves, barely enough to acknowledge that they understand Imogen is Fidele. Our attention is immediately drawn back to Cymbeline, whose speech still sounds cold against the passion of Leontes or Pericles.

Shakespeare appears to feel a need to satisfy the claims of naturalism in making Cymbeline ask the obvious questions, but his concern for dramatic effect quickly re-establishes itself as Cymbeline is used to direct the audience's attention to Posthumus's loving gaze on Imogen. In markedly compressed verse, Cymbeline describes the joyful looks between some of the key partakers of Jupiter's delight.

To what extent the actors' skill in mutely conveying the emotions can compensate for the lack of poetic articulation is very difficult to say. In the theatre, word is supposed to be king, yet there is something uncharacteristically clumsy in Shakespeare's use of Cymbeline to guide the audience's response here. In contrast, we observed earlier, in *Pericles*, how a similar absence of naturalistic dialogue during Thaisa's recognition of Pericles did not detract from the dramatic impact. What we can conclude from this is that although, as in *Pericles*, the numbers and grouping on stage coax the audience out of the auditorium to join with the stage audience, the focus on Cymbeline is at odds with our experience of the rest of the play. Posthumus and Imogen have steered our empathy throughout, and the limited involvement they have in the final act of *Cymbeline*, substantially inhibits our emotional investment in the play.

4

The Winter's Tale

Estrangement and Family Disruption

The Winter's Tale is another play of broken families occasioned by
sexual jealousy at court. Leontes' rampant jealousy finds the confirmation it expects when Polixenes flees Sicilia with his own personal
adviser and friend, Camillo. Before his assembled court he rails
against Hermione, his wife, and in a few terrible moments utterly
destroys his own family. The kernel of this discord is the same
powerful emotional issue that haunts the parting between Posthumus
and Imogen, sexual fidelity. Utterly convinced of Hermione's infidelity by the flight of Camillo and Polixenes, Leontes can no longer
remain silent and passive. When Leontes first turns on his wife with,
'I am glad you did not nurse him' (2.i.56), the audience is fully aware
of what is happening, but Hermione's 'What is this? Sport?' (l. 58)
shows she is simply baffled. Shakespeare permits Leontes to unleash
his anger in as public an arena as possible. Apart from the dark pun he
makes on Hermione's 'sport', stark, direct terms are used to describe
his feelings, so that 'big' and 'swell' become remarkably ugly adjectives in his crudely unambiguous accusation. His accusation is one
sentence, urged on by enjambement, yet he needs to repeat a command to remove Mamillius. Why does he need to repeat himself?
Clearly the onlookers are every bit as shocked and baffled as Hermione.

Hermione's denial is disbelieving rather than assertive. She thinks
so highly of her husband that merely her statement of her innocence

would normally have been enough for him to dismiss any other evidence he might have had. So incredulous is she, that Leontes immediately calls everyone's attention to it with, 'Look on her, mark her well' (l. 65), because her demeanour is so obviously innocent. In *Pericles* and *Cymbeline*, language is often very direct and simple, and characterisation is sacrificed to narrative demands. Here we have verse very similar in type to that we might be familiar with from the lips of Shakespeare's tragic heroes. It is psychologically true and significant in terms of characterisation as Leontes is given the disturbingly believable words of a profoundly sexually jealous man, staggered by his wife's convincing claim to innocence. Having declared her guilty, Leontes did not expect to meet such sound opposition and finds himself alone amidst a sea of incredulous faces. It is a subtle but vital dramatic emphasis.

In the late plays, there are significant differences as well as similarities, and for the critic interested in genre, these differences are amongst the most difficult features to account for. Why is it that in *Pericles* we find little at all that we could comfortably term realistic characterisation, yet in *The Winter's Tale*, as here with Leontes, we find far more?

Leontes' absolute conviction is met by Hermione's measured integrity. The hyperbole she uses in describing 'The most replenish'd villain in the world' (l. 79) as being doubly villainous merely for accusing her, is highly effective in her defence and frustrates Leontes further. She even gives him an easy way out of his public dilemma with her gracious suggestion that he has simply made a mistake, but Leontes toys grimly with her words to re-accuse her, 'You have mistook, my lady, / Polixenes for Leontes' (ll. 81–2). What follows is wholly credible in terms of a sexually jealous mind abruptly freed from inhibitions. Leontes rejects Hermione's regal title in case he should be used as a precedent by others intent on denying the differences in degree between 'the prince and the beggar', a scale which lay at the core of Renaissance political harmony. But the direction of his speech changes where he resorts to his own status, and repetition, to convince the still doubtful faces surrounding him, 'I have said / She's an adultress; I have said with whom' (ll. 87–8), before fuelling his attack with accusations of treachery, a crime of

great import to Jacobean sensibility. Yet such is Shakespeare's understanding of the jealous mind that he makes Leontes indulge his own
sense of injury, and the ornately ugly phrase 'bed-swerver' (l. 93)
emerges from the darker depths of Leontes' feverish imagination.

Hermione's forceful 'No, by my life, / Privy to none of this'
(ll. 95–6) is obviously said to the entire court, while in contrast the
subsequent words are for her husband, as the endearment 'Gentle my
lord' (l. 98) suggests. When intimacy fails, and Leontes not only
demands her arrest, but threatens anyone who speaks for her, Hermione accepts her fate with gracious resignation, blaming the stars
and turning once more to the assembled court to say her farewells.
And it is here that we find the high ideals and elevated behaviour
common to the late plays. Hermione eschews the tears common to
her sex, calling them 'vain dew' (l. 109), then cleverly and paradoxically turns the convention on its head by speaking of a grief 'which
burns / Worse than tears drown' (ll. 111–12) before wholly acquies-
cing to her husband's ill will.

The assembled court appears not only struck dumb, but brought
to a standstill by events, since Leontes has to issue a hopelessly ironic,
rhetorical question, 'Shall I be heard?' (l. 115), instead of a command.
Hermione's departing words again highlight her calm, almost martyr-
like resignation. Their rhythm is gentle and unhurried. Replete with
unshakeable innocence, Hermione tries to find some meaning in
what is happening to her and can only do so by believing that in
the end it will in some way benefit her, 'this action I now go on / Is
for my better grace' (ll. 121–2). But she reserves her final, stingingly
simple speech for her husband, a speech of such confidence and
clarity, it outwits all of Leontes' jealous ranting:

> Adieu, my lord:
> I never wish'd to see you sorry; now
> I trust I shall. My women, come; you have leave.
>   (2.i.122–4)

Like Posthumus, Hermione uses 'Adieu' because she expects to see
her partner again. Like Imogen, Hermione places her 'trust' in time.
She has no doubt that, in time, her innocence will be proved and

when that time comes, she knows precisely how sorry her husband will be. It is not surprising after such an exhibition of dignified suffering that it is in effect Hermione who issues the command to her waiting women, and she who exerts authority, 'come; you have leave' (l. 124).

In this episode we witness from Hermione a quite extraordinary demonstration of patience and courage in the face of terrible suffering. Other characters in the late plays are equally ill treated by fate, or by those they love or those who despise them, and show equal courage and stability. One of the most significant features the four plays have in common is this eagerness to show humanity at its best.

Flight and Foreigners

Although Polixenes has to flee for his life to escape Leontes' murderous wrath, his flight takes him home to Bohemia and not into the insecurity of a foreign court. Flight is all that is left to Polixenes when he discovers that his childhood friend and political ally is the victim of a jealous heart. When Leontes asks Camillo to murder Polixenes, he chooses his assassin badly since it is Camillo who warns Polixenes and advises him to flee without delay.

Camillo initially makes some discreet references to Leontes' jealousy but realises he has to abandon all subterfuge and explain fully. Camillo's advice is clearly singled out by a caesura, which launches him into his account with the words, 'Therefore mark my counsel' (1.ii.408), a phrase reminiscent of Pericles' 'Attend me then' when discussing Antioch with Helicanus. Shakespeare uses strong, clear indicators to guide the pace and tone of the dialogue, but there is a subtle difference between Camillo's words and Pericles'. Whereas Pericles is going to relate a story to Helicanus, Camillo is going to urge immediate action. Appropriately, then, 'Attend me then' comes at the start of a line and is followed by a strong caesura before the tale begins. In contrast, 'Therefore mark my counsel' comes after the caesura, in a speech where the prevalent enjambement demands fluency, so that Camillo can continue to speak almost breathlessly because what he has to say will involve them both in immediate flight.

This urgency is picked up by Polixenes. Instead of lengthy speeches, they exchange rapid half-lines that add to the atmosphere of danger and secrecy. Polixenes' outrage at the idea that he has committed adultery with Hermione is marked. The predominance of images of infection seems fitting when juxtaposed with the nature of Leontes' jealousy, which the audience has witnessed striking him down like some virulent disease. (*Othello* too, of course, contains similar language.) One image is particularly rewarding on closer inspection. Polixenes suggests that if he is guilty, let him be forever associated with Judas Iscariot, the betrayer of Christ (ll. 418–19). In the Jacobean mind of the day, Protestant or Catholic, there is no greater traitor. Polixenes has found the ultimate example, and of course he has done so because he is Leontes' friend. The act of betrayal is as heinous here as the act of adultery.

Yet Camillo knows that Polixenes' outrage is both futile and a waste of precious time. However forcefully Polixenes might claim innocence, Leontes will not be dissuaded from his view. Camillo's use of the phrase 'Swear his thought over' (l. 424) acknowledges, but simultaneously dismisses as pointless, Polixenes' outraged tone. He tells him plainly that that kind of response will prove utterly ineffectual against Leontes' 'faith' (l. 430), something only Polixenes' death could undo. Camillo's speech is an impressive piece of rhetoric that effectively puts a stop to Polixenes' protestations and moves him on, safely and sensibly, to consider what should be done.

Asked 'How should this grow?' (l. 431), as though Polixenes is already resigned to the situation, Camillo launches into what is evidently a pre-arranged plan, pausing only to drive home the necessity for flight. He does not embellish his speech with unnecessary imagery apart from the subservient reference to himself as 'this trunk' (l. 435). He merely tells us what is going to happen. Polixenes is to escape tonight; Camillo will alert his followers and engineer their escape from the city gates; Camillo himself has placed himself in such mortal danger by this breach of confidence, that he will need Polixenes' protection; and he concludes with another piece of skilful diplomatic rhetoric. Should Polixenes display any doubt or hesitation,

Camillo himself will flee, since Polixenes' life is already as forfeit as one not merely condemned to death by the king, but sworn to it.

Simplicity and directness are evident in Polixenes' reply, 'I do believe thee' (l. 446), yet some critics complain of the cowardice Polixenes exhibits, and the casual manner in which Hermione is treated. However, Polixenes does not merely agree with Camillo, in spite of the latter's rhetorical skill and ability as a diplomat. Polixenes adds Camillo's wisdom to the evidence of his own eyes, 'I saw his heart in's face' (l. 447), and why should the audience disbelieve him if they, too, have seen Leontes' heart in his face, and further, been privy to his most private thoughts? Time and time again, critical objections or issues can be made to yield remarkably easily to an analysis of the poetry informed by an imaginative sense of what is happening on stage. There need be no issue here as long as the audience has been witness to Leontes' jealousy in all its subtlety, from its onset, and then hears the finality and decision in Polixenes' words before the caesura in line 447, immediately followed by the powerful dramatic gesture which goes with the words 'Give me thy hand.' We are given the clearest signal possible that Polixenes has embraced Camillo's suggestion by this action, which, with the words, 'Be pilot to me, and thy places shall / Still neighbour mine' (ll. 448–9), binds them together in life or death.

To successfully defend him further against the critical charges levelled at him, Polixenes makes three lucid points, all in defence of his decision to flee.

> This jealousy
> Is for a precious creature: as she's rare,
> Must it be great.
>
> (1.ii.451–3)

He admits he is, like everyone else in this play except Leontes, in awe of Hermione. Her good qualities impress all those around her and that is, in essence, what Polixenes recognises here. Hermione is such an admirable wife, mother and queen, and jealousy such an intensely defensive, selfish passion, that Leontes has a great deal more than most men to defend. The jealousy a woman of Hermione's immense virtue provokes is understandably far more potent and destructive than that of a lesser mortal. His second point, that because Leontes is a powerful monarch, any revenge he seeks in the grip of jealous emotions will be savage indeed, is most interesting since there is a popular critical view that Leontes is not a powerful king but is easily bullied in his own court, for example by Paulina. His final point may be something of a gloss to his second, but from Polixenes' point of view it is an especially strong reason for him to leave as quickly as possible. Because Leontes believes that he has been cuckolded by a loyal, close friend, his revenge will be harsher and more cruel than otherwise. There is both knowledge (of Leontes' character) and wisdom in Polixenes' words, and all three points combine to provide ample reason why escape is the only way to preserve his life, a dilemma common to a number of significant characters in the late plays, and already explored in *Pericles* and *Cymbeline*.

Nonetheless, the following lines from Polixenes' have met with a barrage of critical speculation, and their intransigence is a key cause of critical controversy:

> Fear o'ershades me:
> Good expedition be my friend, and comfort
> The gracious queen, part of his theme, but nothing
> Of his ill-ta'en suspicion!
>
> (1.ii.457–60)

Polixenes concludes his list of dangerous points by admitting to being in fear of his life, then wishes for a speedy and safe escape, which he believes may bring some comfort to Hermione, who, although crucially mixed up in Leontes' jealousy, is utterly innocent. What raises the critical temperature here is how Shakespeare links Polixenes' flight to Hermione's welfare. In other words, how can his safe escape be of any comfort to her? If we bear in mind what we have noted so far, and add to it the image Polixenes first uses to describe his feelings, 'Fear o'ershades me,' it is his own life and fate which is the prime concern throughout. This is not necessarily selfishness. Camillo has confided in him to save *his* life, not Hermione's. As yet, no one can know how Leontes plans to deal with her, and the shock which ripples through the court when he does accuse her of infidelity suggests the idea that she might be in some danger would have been very difficult to believe. Everything that is said about Hermione by others places her firmly beyond reproach, and it is therefore quite credible that, speaking as a friend to Leontes and Hermione, Polixenes would think that his safe escape might comfort Hermione, without his perceiving her to be in mortal danger.

The rhythmical stress which falls on 'nothing' (l. 459) also suggests Polixenes is consciously comparing their dilemmas. Whereas he is so dangerously under Leontes' suspicion that his life is in danger, Hermione is as yet only 'part of his theme'. Polixenes is perhaps even relieved that this is so and thinks of Hermione as safe within the confines of her sympathetic court. All of this rings even truer when Polixenes ends his speech by yet again referring to his own safety, the theme which has dominated the stage for the past few minutes, 'I will respect thee as a father if / Thou bear'st my life off. Hence! let us avoid' (ll. 461–2).

In a foreign land nothing, even the most stable of friendships, is certain, and even the most powerful figure is vulnerable. Polixenes and Pericles resolve this problem by hasty and urgent flight, once more suggesting how the romances dramatise a world subject to change and the irrational actions of human beings.

New Identities

In the latter half of *The Winter's Tale*, disguise is ubiquitous. For Pericles and Imogen, new identities are a means to survive. What advantages do the characters in *The Winter's Tale* gain from adopting a disguise, knowingly or otherwise?

The sheep-shearing feast that introduces us to Perdita and Florizel in Act 4 opens with a whole gaggle of characters entering in groups, and with Camillo and Polixenes having been seen in different costumes up until now, the audience's attention is inevitably drawn to identity from the start. It was common practice in Elizabethan and Jacobean theatre for actors to play more than one role, and if we take that into account, it is clear that, until they spoke, Camillo and

Polixenes could have been anyone as far as the audience was concerned.

Florizel's opening speech highlights the issue of identity and is richly ironic, in that although he is himself enjoying the freedom of his illicit disguise, and describes Perdita as one of 'the petty gods' (4.iv.4) and 'the queen' (l. 5) of the feast, unlike the audience he has no idea she really is a princess. She, in contrast, is extremely aware of her fancy dress and of its unsuitability. From the moment she speaks, Perdita is firmly stamped as a heroine of the late plays. For a shepherdess, in spite of her own protests, she speaks eloquently. She addresses Florizel formally and with a sophisticated sense of his role in the social order. She also knows her own place and chides herself for chiding him, interrupting herself for being impudent:

> To chide at your extremes, it not becomes me –
> O pardon that I name them! Your high self.
>
> (4.iv.6–7)

Although Perdita possesses great beauty, it goes hand in hand with great humility. Indeed, the whole tenor of her demeanour is one of humility. For Perdita, not only is she undeserving of Florizel's extreme attentions, but he lowers himself by dressing as a shepherd.

The syntax she employs is also quite sophisticated. The single sentence beginning 'Your high self' (l. 7) is sustained for a further eight lines, and there is a skilful balance between the verbs 'blush' and 'swoon' at the end. Like Imogen, Perdita appears to find the whole business of dressing up uncomfortable and awkward. There is no way she can be accused here of any sort of false modesty; she *feels* wrong. Imogen, Marina and Perdita embody some extreme qualities. Their virtue is unassailable and even this light-hearted, liberating game of dressing-up makes them uneasy. If we are tempted at this point to find our sympathy slipping away from Perdita, to see her caution as prudish, prissy or even unreal, we have to keep a firm hold on the historical and social context of the period. Perdita herself immediately provides it.

Florizel relates to us the history of their meeting as briefly as it is possible to do, and his use of 'bless' hints at a divine intervention that

Perdita latches onto. 'Now Jove afford you cause!' (l. 16) she exclaims, stressing that she, too, wishes the gods to look kindly on their
relationship. Florizel, like Imogen, has a regal habit of command and
he has therefore 'not been us'd to fear' (l. 18), but Perdita understands that the social gulf existing between them is an insuperable
barrier and uses the word 'dread' (l. 17) with good reason. She knows
that their relationship, even though pure and chaste, contravenes a
hierarchy linking the gods to the King, and to his son. She also knows
that it is perfectly possible for Polixenes to stumble on them as
Florizel did her, but even her anxiety is infused with humility and
she places Florizel's safety before her own, which adds to our view of
her as noble and yet humble. It is a combination shared by Miranda
and Marina, and there is a distinct similarity in the way all three speak.

Despite its festive trappings, the sheep-shearing scene immediately
shifts into a serious, private discussion between the two young lovers,
and Florizel now does what he can to lessen Perdita's fears. This is a
festive occasion and Perdita is after all the central figure. Florizel also
employs a detailed analogy, reminding Perdita that the Gods themselves have adopted human form for love, which ought to be a persuasive argument to use with Perdita because of its dependence on
godly humility. Complimenting his lover profoundly, Florizel adds,
'Their transformations / Were never for a piece of beauty rarer'
(ll. 31–2), but then immediately throws cold water on his ardour by
asserting his own chaste desires. Why, we might ask, does he suddenly make a statement about his honourable intentions? Is it necessary for us to know that Perdita is a virgin? It is the kind of statement
that strikes modern audiences as quaint or even foolish, but to try
and evade it or even omit it, as some modern productions do, is to
ignore the way the verse works. Shakespeare's audience, however ill
or well educated, would have known that all the examples of godly
transformation Florizel gives are rooted more in lust, resulting in
rape, than in virtuous love. It is entirely logical, then, that he should
rapidly counter his risky analogy by saying that in contrast, his love is
entirely chaste.

But Florizel's claim is not only a very logical response to his own
rash analogy, it is also a means of affirming Perdita's virtuous power
– something, given the background of her conception and birth, that

Shakespeare is eager to do if Leontes' family is to be happily reunited. However jolly and liberated this sheep-shearing festival is, whatever musical or dance resources a production employs, it would emasculate one of the play's chief aims if any intimation at all were created that Perdita and Florizel were adult, sexual partners. The late plays have a common belief in the ultimate good of the family, its unity and happiness. In his tragedies Shakespeare explored in some detail the consequences of familial corruption or conflict, most obviously in *Hamlet* and *King Lear*, but in the late plays he replaces the tragic ending with reconciliations full of joy and harmony. Such a reconciliation would be impossible if Perdita's virtue was in doubt.

Perdita again exhibits a sophistication way beyond her adopted role as shepherd's daughter when she disputes Florizel's vow of honourable constancy. She says clearly and simply that once confronted by his father, who is of course also the King, Florizel cannot maintain his determination to marry her, but it is her subsequent conclusion that most reveals her level of intelligence. She knows that either Florizel must abandon his purpose of marrying her, or she must abandon her life as a shepherdess to become his wife. It is her choice of words and expression which are revealing, and which tie her so strongly into the late-play heroine mould. Using the one verb 'change' to apply to two objects, 'purpose' and 'life' (rhetorically, a simple use of syllepsis), she creates a striking antithesis. Instantly she makes Florizel, and us, see how much harder it is to change a 'life':

> One of these two must be necessities,
> Which then will speak, that you must change this purpose,
> Or I my life.

> (4.iv.38–40)

Marina too has this rhetorical gift, and uses it most noticeably in her conversion of Lysimachus as well as in her reconciliatory conversation with Pericles.

Florizel's concluding contribution to the lovers' debate is full of honest simplicity, the core of which is his open-hearted claim that

For I cannot be
Mine own, nor anything to any, if
I be not thine.

(4.iv.43–5)

As elsewhere in the late plays, here we have a kind of dramatic
shorthand. Florizel is not given the opportunity to woo Perdita;
there is no time for courtship or passion. Yet it is vital that we
believe in his love for her and in his honourable treatment of her.
Shakespeare's solution is to substitute simplicity for eloquence because he knows it can be equally convincing. To wear one's heart on
one's sleeve is perhaps risky, but it is also persuasive, and Florizel is
the epitome of the guileless lover. We are not permitted the least
space to doubt him.

Having assured Perdita of his love, he then suggests she divert her
gloomy thoughts with anything that amuses her at the feast, and adds
that she has a responsibility to be merry for the guests. His final
encouragement, to smile as though it were their wedding day, meets
Perdita's approval since she, too, has abandoned her fate to destiny,
but however keenly Perdita prays, the lovers soon find themselves
forced to flee and seek safety in a foreign land, and new disguises
form a part of that plan. Florizel exchanges clothes with Autolycus,
and Perdita is falsely presented at Leontes' court as a Libyan princess
as well as Florizel's wife. This foregrounds one very obvious but
significant observation about this issue of identity in the late plays.
Whatever the necessity, however exigent the moment, any new
identity or disguise is inherently temporary. Shakespeare's characters
cannot, as Perdita intimates in her discussion with Florizel, ultimately
change their lives. They may rediscover a life lost, but they can never
manufacture a stable, new identity.

Trials and Tests

Possibly the harshest trial undergone by any of the characters is that
endured by Hermione in *The Winter's Tale*. The list of cruelties
inflicted by Leontes, his perception of reality warped by a ferocious

sexual jealousy, on those closest to him is extraordinary. He plots to kill his friend Polixenes and attempts to use his most honourable counsellor, Camillo, to do it. He separates his young son Mamillius from his mother; he then imprisons Hermione even though she is about to give birth and when she does, he has the baby abandoned on a distant shore to ensure its death. If that were not enough, he drags his wife, almost straight from her childbed, to face his lurid accusations in a formal court.

After defending herself with admirable calm in two lengthy, supremely rational speeches, Hermione is at a loss what more she can say and resigns herself to her fate in an image drawn from shooting: 'My life stands in the level of your dreams' (3.ii.81). To 'level' is to aim a gun, and she is so painfully aware of the irrational nature of Leontes' behaviour, that she knows she cannot combat it. His 'dreams' do indeed control her fate, and it is that word which Shakespeare makes Leontes grasp in his furious response. As in *Othello* and *Cymbeline*, in *The Winter's Tale* Shakespeare shows a profound understanding of what jealousy is and how it operates on the male psyche. The apparently rhetorical accusation, 'Your actions are my dreams' (3.ii.82), is a skilful use of dramatic irony. While attempting to enforce his own version of reality by stating that Hermione is trying to evade punishment by calling her actions 'dreams', he exposes the stark reality of his own jealousy. Hermione's imagined sexual acts do, indeed, fill Leontes' dreams, which is why he has been moved to take such dreadful actions himself.

The caesura in line 84, 'And I but dream'd it! As you were past all shame', underlines the rhetoric. Leontes expects his own shocked tone to convey the absurdity of what Hermione contends. His intemperate language is also in marked contrast to Hermione's quiet reason. It continues as he asserts that adulteresses, as they are immune to shame, are naturally incapable of truth, and that by denying the crime, Hermione is only digressing and cannot ultimately avoid his justice. His justice is overtly presented as a threat. Just as the child has felt the sting of Leontes' justice, so will the mother, although in her case there is the added implication of torture that comes with, 'in whose easiest passage / Look for no less than death' (ll. 90–1). Death is the least that can happen to Hermione.

Physically and psychologically weakened, Hermione is exposed not only to her husband's devastating cruelty, but to the winter weather and the gaze of the assembled court. Her remarkably heroic behaviour unites her with other heroines of the late plays, who all exhibit an admirably stoical response to the most vindictive twists of fate.

In repudiating his threats, Hermione nonetheless remains dutiful and formal, maintaining the rational, measured tone which is the hallmark of her defence in this trial. But in denying death's power over her, she also shocks us by wishing for it. Life has no advantage – 'commodity' (l. 93) – when bereft of all those things that for her give it meaning. These she places in a list and, as usual in Shakespeare, a list with a meaningful structure. In keeping with Hermione's queenly grace, the first of her losses is her husband's love, which Hermione describes appropriately as the 'crown and comfort of my life' (l. 95). Though unable to understand the processes of jealousy that have caused her to lose Leontes' love, Hermione stresses her own sense of utter deprivation, 'for I do feel it gone' (l. 95). Second in significance is the separation from her son Mamillius, from whom she is 'barr'd, like one infectious' (l. 98). The choice of adjective clearly echoes Shakespeare's broader understanding of jealousy and its *modus oper-andi*. Thirdly, she has lost her newborn daughter, who has been 'Hal'd out to murder' (l. 101), and again Hermione chooses a word which stresses the violence and unnaturalness of Leontes' behaviour. Fourth in the list is that Hermione has been publicly accused of being a whore; and fifth, that she has not even been allowed time to recover from the birth, a kindness belonging to even the poorest woman. Denied even natural convalescence, she has herself been dragged to this outdoor, winter scene, to be tried. In contrast to Leontes' earlier attempt to indict Hermione, this list indicts Leontes with increasing force and effect, making her rhetorical conclusion,

> Now, my liege,
> Tell me what blessings I have here alive,
> That I should fear to die?
>
> (3.ii.106–8)

irrefutable. The caesura makes Hermione appear to wait for an answer, and when even Leontes cannot respond, she continues, 'Therefore proceed' (l. 108).

At this moment Shakespeare surprises his stage and his real audience. Hermione's powerful list has successfully quelled even Leontes' riotous imagination but instead of allowing the trial to continue, Hermione adds one final proviso and appeals to all present, actors and audience, to hear her. The gravity of her pronouncement is conveyed by two curt, imperative phrases, before she reminds them all that it is not her life she seeks, but her honour. Hermione's determination to protect her good name is, of course, what we should expect of any heroine in the late plays. Fidelity is regarded as a crucial foundation for the relationships that these plays construct, test, destroy and rebuild. Marina goes to astounding lengths to protect her own chastity. Hermione proclaims her own innocence and places her trust in the gods, as represented by the oracle from Apollo. Her innocence gives her the confidence to assert that there can be no tangible evidence or proof.

By putting her trust in Apollo, she is also placing herself out of Leontes' reach and he is rendered incapable of a response. It is an attendant Lord who voices what all watchers are thinking, 'This your request / Is altogether just' (ll. 116–17), before calling for the Oracle to judge Hermione and Leontes.

The trial proceeds to the next stage, the formal presentation of the Oracle, and Leontes is made to re-establish contact with the outside world, formally ordering the break-up of the seals. Shakespeare chose to follow his source, *Pandosto*, for the actual wording of the Oracle, which interestingly flies in the face of dramatic convention. Oracular pronouncements are conventionally enigmatic. This one could not be more blunt. The brevity of the immediate responses from Lords and Hermione are interesting indications of how much tension Shakespeare built into this scene. There is no luxurious wallowing in righteousness from anyone, merely a palpable sense of relief on behalf of the victimised Hermione. Shakespeare's skill is again evident in the immediate counter-action. The audience has barely had time to breathe before Leontes denies the Oracle and, in so doing, commits an act of hubris that brings possibly the swiftest divine justice in theatrical history. Before anyone can react to Leontes' appallingly sacrilegious demand, a servant enters in a state of panic to announce that Mamillius, anticipating the fate of his mother, is dead. In disbelief, Leontes can only utter the futile 'How! Gone?' (l. 145) while Hermione finally succumbs to the extremes of her position and collapses the moment her husband recognises Apollo's anger and his own guilt.

It is at this point that Paulina intervenes to take charge of Hermione, as we later discover, but in doing so she, too, points to the gods and highlights Leontes' guilt. The audience has no reason to distrust Paulina, and the trial ends with Hermione's apparent death. When we consider what she has undergone, the quite remarkable degree of suffering Shakespeare has generated for her, it is hardly surprising. We might think that, as with Lear, 'The wonder is [she] hath endured so long.'

Time and Tide

In *The Winter's Tale*, time's part in bringing about a shift in circumstances and events favouring reconciliation is orchestrated by Paulina. At the start of the final act, Leontes is discovered in discussion with his nobles about the fate of his throne. Paulina plays a central role and there are important questions to ask about her tone and manner. Is she angry or conciliatory? Does she exert influence over Leontes easily or is she constrained to argue?

Cleomenes opens Act 5, Scene i, confident that Leontes has done more than enough penance, and encourages his master to forget and forgive himself. Leontes' response is fundamental to the whole relationship between time and suffering. He is simply unable to forget. In these plays time never eradicates the pain of loss or cruelty of circumstance. As Belarius's cynical view of the court in *Cymbeline* (3.iii.44–64) made clear, that is not the way that time heals. Time allows for reflection, and reflection in turn leads the wise man to greater knowledge. It leads Leontes to a complete acknowledgement of the role jealousy played in Hermione's death:

> Whilst I remember
> Her, and her virtues, I cannot forget
> My blemishes in them, and so still think of
> The wrong I did myself: which was so much,
> That heirless it hath made my kingdom, and
> Destroy'd the sweet'st companion that e'er man
> Bred his hopes out of.
>
>   (5.i.7–13)

Not only has he endangered the kingdom, leaving it heirless, but he has destroyed his own peace and joy. Shakespeare brings the private loss and the state's loss together by referring to Hermione as wife and mother.

Paulina's emphasis is different. As guardian of the still living Hermione and keeper of faith in the oracle, she concentrates on the Queen. It is Hermione's absolute perfection she insists on. Cleverly, she suggests that even if Leontes was to marry every woman in the world, or from every woman take something good to make a perfect whole, he still could not match the woman he has lost. But we began this section with questions about Paulina's tone, and the opening and closing phrases of her speech are extremely pointedly chosen in this respect. 'True, too true, my lord' (l. 12) respectfully confirms Leontes' own idea without leaving room for doubt at all. It is a clichéd expression that acknowledges a sad but unavoidable truth, but also closes debate. There is a similar use of rhetoric in her phrase 'she you kill'd' (l. 15). Where tact might dictate she at least use a euphemism, necessity dictates otherwise. Paulina's intention is to keep Leontes from considering remarrying and therefore she must counter any such suggestion from nobles like Cleomenes. This becomes obvious when Paulina's choice of words is openly criticised by Cleomenes; but she ignores his rebuke for the more pertinent point that he is more interested in convincing Leontes that he should remarry.

That the issue of an heir has become of great concern to Leontes' court is now made very clear as Dion counters Paulina's view with one of his own, in which the health of the state figures centrally. But as we repeatedly see in these plays, Shakespeare's royal protagonists are first and foremost fathers and daughters, wives and sons. In dramatic terms what we experience as members of an audience we feel on their behalf, not on behalf of some transferred sense of national identity.

Paulina responds to Dion's rational logic by reaffirming Hermione's absolute perfection, but in his appeal to divinity he also gives Paulina the cue to remind the court and audience of the oracle and its insistence that Leontes will remain heirless until his lost daughter be found. Her subsequent point that remarriage would oppose the will of Apollo is wholly unassailable and the dramatic effect is to persuade Leontes to her will. Time has taught him the truth of Paulina's words, which is why he agrees with her so readily and even states that if he had listened to her in the first place Hermione might still be alive.

It is because both Leontes and Paulina are speaking with the understanding of emotion, not of reason, that they can combine in the way they then do in imagining Hermione's ghost haunting him for choosing a new bride. The other nobles appear excluded from this exchange, both dramatically and by experience, and Paulina's vivid image of Hermione's ghost demanding to know why she has been so insulted, wrings an emotional outburst from Leontes that quashes further debate.

Having won the argument, Paulina demands public acknowledgement of her victory, and the level of emotion attained is indicated by Cleomenes' 'You tempt him over-much' (l. 73) and his polite attempt at a rebuke, 'Good madam', as she continues to prepare the ground for the reconciliation she has so carefully designed. There is something undoubtedly comical, and in keeping with Paulina's truculent character, in her insistence, after such a fierce refusal of the possibility, that should he insist on marrying, he must let her choose his bride for him. But it enables her to provide us with the dramatic paradox she is waiting to resolve:

> That
> Shall be when your first queen's again in breath:
> Never till then.

> (5.i.82–3)

The penitent Leontes we have observed in this scene is a remarkable contrast with the jealous tyrant who raged at Antigonus for his failure to control his harridan of a wife. It has taken sixteen years of daily prayer and ritual mourning to scour Leontes' jealous heart clean enough to bring the saintly Hermione back within its compass.

Unusually, in this play Time is actually given a dramatic role and appears at the start of Act 4 as a chorus to assist the audience in making the substantial shift from a Sicilia ravaged by Leontes' jealousy, to a Bohemia governed by pastoral harmony, leaping the sixteen years it has taken Perdita to reach a marriageable age. This links the play closely with both *Pericles* and *The Tempest*, where the time taken for the protagonist's daughter to become nubile is a central issue since it allows the possibility of renewal and regeneration through marriage and an extended family. Apart from this more recognisably conventional dramatic function, Time has some intriguing comments to make on his relationship with humanity:

> I that please some, try all: both joy and terror
> Of good and bad, that makes and unfolds error,
> Now take upon me, in the name of Time,
> To use my wings.
>
>   (4.i.1–4)

Time's involvement in human affairs is so overwhelming as to be almost godlike yet paradoxically he is also, unlike the other gods that people the late plays, markedly neutral. Shakespeare personifies him here, rather like Gower in *Pericles*, more as a disinterested commentator than an involved participant. The list of antitheses, 'some, try all', 'joy and terror', 'good and bad', and 'makes and unfolds', stress this neutrality. Nonetheless, Time's power is undoubtedly godlike since he adds:

>   since it is in my power
> To o'erthrow law, and in one self-born hour
> To plant and o'erwhelm custom.
>
>   (4.i.7–9)

This is entirely in keeping with the audience's experience of these plays, where joy and misery keep such close company, and the speed of change sometimes appears so unnatural as to render them difficult plays to realise. In truth what Shakespeare is doing is faithfully reflecting the extreme possibilities of human experience, another strong reason to accept that the late plays do genuinely reflect a mature stage in his dramatic art and a demonstrable development of the theatre which preceded them.

Suffering and Forgiveness

The suffering inflicted on Leontes in *The Winter's Tale* comes with such near-absurd speed and weight that he loses his son and wife within moments of his hubristic denial of the oracle's truth. Immediately following his blatant and unambiguously worded denial of Apollo's oracle, a servant enters, sufficiently breathless and agitated to earn an impatient response from Leontes who is still engrossed in his jealous abuse of Hermione. The servant reports Mamillius's death in the conventional manner, anxious for his own safety as the bearer of bad news, but adds the important detail that the cause of the child's death was fear for his mother. Leontes can only stammer forth 'How! gone?' (3.ii.144) in disbelief, before receiving the unequivocal reply 'Is dead.' Sometimes such abrupt demises tempt modern directors to seek means to lessen what they perceive as an awkward dramatic moment that strains the audience's credibility. Editing becomes an excuse for a failure to understand the text fully. Leontes has absolutely no difficulty understanding his son's death. Instantly he says:

> Apollo's angry, and the heavens themselves
> Do strike at my injustice.
>
> (3.ii.146–7)

He uses the word 'strike' to describe what he sees as an act of instant correction, when more neutral words are freely available. He *knows* this death is unnatural. Paulina, too, thinks this way because when

Hermione faints, she doesn't hesitate herself in anticipating Hermione's fate and in seeing death at work. Paulina doesn't doubt Hermione's collapse is fatal, and to interpose suggestions that this is part of some plot of hers is to misunderstand the nature of the romance genre. Leontes makes it even clearer that he understands he is being punished when, after giving instructions for Hermione to be looked after, he immediately sets about seeking pardon in the only way he knows.

Leontes' plea for forgiveness contains not only a list of his good intentions, but a list of his transgressions as well. Compared with Posthumus's soul searching in *Cymbeline*, it might appear crude, but it is nonetheless human for that. Posthumus has the luxury of being alone with his thoughts and his God, while Leontes' guilt is a matter of public show. His rush of contrition is also motivated by a desire to appease the gods before they punish him further, something he appears to fail to do, but in effect genuinely achieves, since Hermione does not die and Paulina's ruse becomes a part of the gods' greater purpose.

Leontes makes the connection between his jealousy and these events himself, and after seeking Apollo's pardon, launches into a desperate attempt to curtail the god's anger, speaking in terrified haste and urgency. First come three actions he promises to take:

> I'll reconcile me to Polixenes,
> New woo my queen, recall the good Camillo.
> (3.ii.155–6)

All three show considerable insight into the nature of his own sins as they have been revealed in the court proceedings against Hermione; Leontes is aware that his jealousy has hurt far more than his queen. Next he admits corrupting Camillo, and blackmailing him into killing Polixenes, a murder he knows would have taken place but for Camillo's impervious moral character. Leontes concludes by comparing himself with Camillo because in that comparison lies the heart of his guilt: where Leontes displayed moral cowardice and weakness, Camillo responded with courage and strength. Leontes' contrite outburst is comprehensive enough, but Paulina's entrance etches it in stone.

Paulina's high degree of distress is clear from her opening outburst of grief, and although it is to Leontes she clearly directs her speech, it is one of the lords who speaks to her first. If we pursue the notion that Leontes is acutely aware of the danger he is in from Apollo, then his silence is not at all surprising since he knows exactly what Paulina is indirectly referring to before she ever mentions Hermione's death. Leontes has just been seen trying desperately to avoid such an eventuality. Paulina's horrified entrance confirms visually what Leontes dreaded: Hermione is dead. What more is there for him to say?

Looked at clinically, Paulina's tirade (ll. 175–214) appears emotional in the extreme. She speaks in brief bursts, heaps together a list of torments and insults, and works herself into such a frenzy that the lord feels moved to admonish her for disrespect. Yet there are some very subtle but crucial qualities here that illuminate Shakespeare's treatment of suffering.

Paulina opens rhetorically with a series of questions, but the rhythm places acute emphases in key places:

> What studied torments, tyrant, hast for me?
> What wheels? racks? fires? what flaying? boiling?
> In leads or oils? What old or newer torture
> Must I receive, whose every word deserves
> To taste of thy most worst?
>
> (3.ii.175–9)

The word 'tyrant' (l. 175), building on the harsh 't' sounds of 'studied torments', is isolated rhythmically. No one present can fail to understand Paulina's accusation from the start. Similarly, the list of tortures that follows has a measured rhythm that is completely counter to the notion that Paulina is out of control. Castigating him for childish weaknesses, Paulina forces him to think of what those weaknesses have actually led to, and behind the admission of Mamillius's death, is the implied death of Hermione. 'Thy by-gone fooleries were but spices of it' (l. 184) leaves the apparently insignificant 'it' echoing hollowly, allowing time for all to ponder before Paulina recommences her attack with an equally calculated list of accusations.

First comes Polixenes. That betrayal Paulina almost dismisses, since all it did was show Leontes to be inconstant as a friend. She regards his treatment of Camillo as almost equally weak and links the two as 'poor trespasses' compared with those she has yet to proclaim. Her rhetorical intent is clearly evident in her use of understatement. His betrayal of Polixenes becomes 'nothing', while to have Camillo murder a king she dismisses as 'nor was't much'. She employs the same technique with Perdita's abandonment, referring to it as 'none or little'. But she begins to work her way towards the terrifying 'it' she has prepared her audience for so adeptly, by adding, 'though a devil / Would have shed water out of fire, ere done 't' (ll. 192–3), reminding all of the ultimate price of sin. Leontes' involvement in Mamillius's death, too, she understates, making it seem in some way a noble act by the child, which disgraces Leontes' own behaviour.

A cursory examination of the final few lines of her speech might suggest that the broken rhythm is indicative of her emotion, whereas in effect it is a wonderfully constructed piece of rhetoric. Her simple 'but the last' she interrupts, to gain the firm attention of her courtly audience, 'O lords, / When I have said, cry "woe!"', while it also allows her to delay the revelation which each man present, including Leontes, knows is coming. Repetition serves to underline the final horror of 'the queen, the queen, / The sweet'st, dear'st creature's dead' (ll. 200–1), before Paulina climaxes her adroit, public condemnation in an incomplete and dully emphatic half-line, 'and vengeance for't / Not dropp'd down yet.'

The underlying reason for her control is, of course, that Paulina is involved in a deceit. Hermione is not dead. Indeed, Paulina is consciously creating the impression that she is, in order to save her life. That this is the case appears to be even hinted at by Shakespeare. When the lord proclaims 'The higher powers forbid!' (l. 202), a rather neutral expression voicing dismay, Paulina responds with a vehement defence of what she has said, as though he has accused her of lying.

However, Shakespeare is also engaged on another purpose in giving Paulina the dominant role he does here, a purpose she instantly returns to, the moment she feels she has quashed any doubt. She denies Leontes the capacity for repentance and urges him to despair. Ironically, her purpose for Shakespeare is the precise opposite of that she states. She seems to be denying the possibility of his ever being forgiven, which is made clear when she adds,

> A thousand knees
> Ten thousand years together, naked, fasting,
> Upon a barren mountain, and still winter
> In storm perpetual, could not move the gods
> To look that way thou wert.
>
> (3.ii.210–14)

Paulina is actually *giving* him the opportunity to seek forgiveness. Indeed, in preserving Hermione's life, Apollo has already responded to the rush of contrition Leontes felt and voiced as soon as Mamillius died. In spite of the plethora of deities involved in the late plays, the nature of that forgiveness – instant, unreserved and dependent only on the true penitence of the sinner – is an entirely Christian one.

Leontes maintains a silence when Paulina first appears and he knows his wife is dead. He listens while his truly terrible sins are listed and publicly catalogued. Is it any surprise, then, that his first words are so contrite and humble, especially after Paulina's skilful exposition of his sinful nature.

> Go on, go on:
> Thou canst not speak too much; I have deserv'd
> All tongues to talk their bitt'rest.
>
> (3.ii.214–16)

At this, the lord intervenes and tries to curb Paulina's tongue but in doing so gives Shakespeare the opportunity to underscore the ideology of suffering and forgiveness which pervades these plays. Free from sin, except perhaps the sin of deceit, which as yet she does not truly regard as a sin in that she feels no guilt, Paulina can state easily and with absolute conviction,

> All faults I make, when I shall come to know them,
> I do repent.
>
> (3.ii.219–20)

Leontes has already come to know his faults, and Paulina has been instrumental in that process of understanding.

Paulina's role often generates critical debate. Why does she now appear to have such a dramatic change of heart, to leap from outrage to calm acceptance? Critics and directors see something awkward, even comic, in the way she continues to goad Leontes, apparently accidentally. This stems from a misunderstanding of the connection between suffering and forgiveness in the late plays. Her speech after Leontes' admission of guilt makes dramatic sense without tinkering with it in any way. It is a far more balanced, calm piece of verse that proceeds in measured, clear sentences rooted in an acute awareness of what is happening to Leontes, the focus of all her dialogue in this scene:

> Alas! I have showed too much
> The rashness of a woman: he is touch'd
> To th' noble heart.
>
> (3.ii.220–2)

Paulina freely acknowledges Leontes' suffering. She admits that her words and the events they have described have caused him immense pain. Paulina knows Leontes will not be able to forget that time is a necessary element in healing, which is why she denied him the chance in an earlier speech which set him on his knees, on a winter mountainside, for ten thousand years. What she is really doing now is giving Leontes the opportunity to speak, and act, for himself. Her whole purpose, up until this point, has been to 'afflict' Leontes and remind him of what he has done. Her suggestion that she be punished merely serves to remind Leontes of his own sinful status. It makes dramatic sense to view Paulina's speech here as wholly dependent on Leontes' reactions. Her rebellious tone abandoned, she speaks respectfully to him, and when she *sees* real grief overtake him again, at the mere mention of Hermione, 'The love I bore your queen – lo, fool again' (l. 228), she digresses momentarily, but instantly returns to her theme to conclude her speech with the strongest hint of all that Leontes' fate is now subject to time, 'take your patience to you, / And I'll say nothing' (ll. 231–2).

Leontes' response is critical in understanding this scene and explains why Shakespeare cannot easily be accused of weakness in his handling of Paulina. Leontes recognises the truth in everything Paulina has said. 'Thou didst speak but well / When most the truth' (ll. 232–3) he says, with chilling honesty, and with a frail remnant of self-respect adds, 'which I receive much better / Than to be pitied of thee' (l. 234). Paulina's rhetoric has done its work well and Leontes begins his long road to restoration via several statements of intent. He will bury his wife and son in one grave and on the headstone inscribe his own guilt for all eternity. Once a day, he will visit the chapel where they are buried where his only recreation will be tears. He will continue this mourning for as long as his physical being will allow him to, and finally, to emphasise the absolute control Paulina has achieved, he gives himself over to her authority, 'Come, and lead me / To these sorrows' (ll. 242–3).

When Leontes leaves the stage, the audience knows he faces years of grief and sorrow, the price of his sin. But equally, they also know that under Paulina's prompting, he has laid the foundation for redemption. As with other of the late plays, suffering, however unbearable, is ultimately slave to time and to repentance.

Divine Magic

The interplay between magic, divinity and death, as in the other late plays, is noticeable in *The Winter's Tale*. Antigonus, instructed to abandon the newborn Perdita by her insanely jealous father, struggles with his own conscience before doing so. When Antigonus checks with the Mariner that they have landed on a remote Bohemian shore, the Mariner is full of foreboding and adds to his description of the coming storm, the conviction that it is divine intervention. Antigonus responds dutifully, 'Their sacred wills be done!' (3.iii.7), ironically unaware of how brief a role he is to play in the gods' greater plan. The Mariner again warns of the impending storm, adding information about the wild animals, to prepare us for Antigonus's infamously bizarre death. As he departs, his simple words underscore the terrible nature of the action Antigonus is about to take. This leaves

Antigonus alone with his thoughts, which Shakespeare conventionally allows him to share with us. This is a wild, remote place, a storm is building even as he speaks, and in his arms he carries a newborn baby.

If Antigonus follows the Mariner's injunction not to stray too far inland, he may walk as he speaks the lines describing his dream, to suggest his progress away from the shore. The dream itself, like Posthumus's, has all the signs of divine intervention, but it starts from a vitally false premise. Antigonus believes Hermione is dead. The audience, with Leontes, has only moments before been informed by Paulina that Hermione has indeed died, but there is a key difference between what Antigonus believes and what the audience knows. They have seen Hermione proved innocent by the oracle, Antigonus has not, and the visitation by her in his dream is his only evidence of her death, which he takes as confirmation of her guilt. Torn though he is between duty and essential humanity, in the end he believes he must do what the gods wish and so announces his intention to leave the bastard daughter of King Polixenes to fend for herself.

But the dream itself dominates his lengthy soliloquy. Antigonus asserts its reality, before realising it for the audience. It is impossible not to picture the woman Antigonus creates, her head tilted one way then another as though in puzzled wonder, her whole figure brimming with sorrow and yet 'sanctity'. His comparison of her to a 'vessel' (3.iii.21) works on several levels. Besides the obvious metaphorical connection implied between 'pure white robes' and sails, we have the idea that Hermione is a 'vessel' overflowing, 'fill'd' with grief, and it is unwise to ignore the divine connotations rooted in Christian usage, where it is a term frequently used either for a holy object like a chalice, or figuratively for that body which houses a divine soul. Hardly surprising, then, that Antigonus draws these images together into the simile 'Like very sanctity' (l. 23) to describe Hermione's approach. Her bowing three times before commencing to speak also adds to the religious aura surrounding the visitation, and while her 'gasping' resounds with realism, the hyperbole of 'her eyes / Became two spouts' (ll. 25–6) is perhaps a little grotesque. Yet both are there to signify the depth of her grief, a grief so powerful, Antigonus calls it 'fury'.

The words that finally 'break' from her are full of narrative simplicity. Hermione in effect christens Perdita, and announces Antigonus's death, a necessity if Perdita is to be truly lost for 16 years. Although her words' primary function is to move the play forward, they also contain some other details worth noting. Hermione specifically frees Antigonus from blame. She calls him 'Good Antigonus' (l. 27) and agrees that he is doing this against his judgement and on an oath of allegiance. The unfortunate Antigonus has no real say in what he does here. He is a tool of the divine will, an insignificant part of a much larger plan, yet Shakespeare refuses to make him conventionally devoid of character or humanity. Instead he gives Antigonus sufficient motivation and purpose to reinforce the sorrow of his task, while providing him with poetry that enhances the tragedy of Hermione's death, and simultaneously ennobles him. In this way he maximises the pathos of this moment, the abandonment of a baby in a desolate region, at the mercy of wild animals and a burgeoning storm.

Hermione's ghost leaves 'with shrieks' and Antigonus remarks that he was so frightened, he believed what he had seen was real. His conclusion, noted earlier, that Hermione is dead and was guilty, has the benefit of absolving him of all personal guilt and steeling him to do what his 'heart bleeds' over. Antigonus's choice of image indicates clearly that he places Perdita on the ground. Yet another mid-line pause draws attention to the action before the wonderfully ironic words, 'Blossom, speed thee well!' (l. 45), provide just the faintest shadow of hope. In spite of the totally inimical natural circumstances, Antigonus grasps at the divine will at work underneath it all and places the helpless child in the lap of the gods. Beside the child he lays a written account of her birth and lineage and the evidence to verify it, plus the money that the shepherd is to find and which is to provide for Perdita's upbringing. The hope that she will survive underpins all these words and actions before the rising storm alerts him to his own danger.

Reminding himself of Hermione's guilt stresses the infant's innocence, yet Antigonus cannot obey Hermione's injunction, 'There weep, and leave it crying' (l. 32). Instead, he outdoes the conventional marks of grief with 'my heart bleeds' and the ironic acknowledgement that he is on oath. Poetry once more comes into play to describe the storm's increase before he famously exits, '*pursued by a bear*'. The vagueness of his departing words,

> A savage clamour!
> Well may I get aboard! This is the chase:
> I am gone forever!
>   (3.iii.56–8)

leaves it very unclear how Antigonus's final few moments were conceived dramatically. Impressive critical energy has been expended over this question, on speculation about whether or not a tame bear was used and what dramatic effect this would have, which leads to the question of how tragic or comic this moment was intended to be. Two simple points deserve to be made. First, Antigonus's ursine departure is immediately succeeded by comedy in the shape of the Shepherd and his son, and secondly, he has said more than enough to convince the audience his death is divinely ordained. It is an unwise director who ignores these basic premises.

Revived Families

The Winter's Tale concludes with one of Shakespeare's most famous *coups de théâtre*, Hermione's transformation from statue to moving flesh and blood. Paulina prepares her triumphant moment, not merely by praising the work of the sculptor, but by linking the statue's perfection to the moral value of the woman it purports to portray. Having reminded both Leontes and the audience of Hermione's moral perfection, Paulina emphasises the moment of revelation by insisting on the statue's verisimilitude *before* she actually reveals it to view.

Among the most difficult things for directors and actors to recognise in Shakespeare's texts, are those moments when silence is more voluble than dialogue. There is no excuse for not allowing sufficient silence and time here for the two audiences, stage and real, to wonder at the object discovered before them, since Paulina's words overtly tell the director what to do. It may seem obvious from a scholarly point of view to state it, but we do need to remind ourselves that as far as the real audience is concerned Hermione died 16 years ago. Paulina relishes her moment of triumph:

> I like your silence, it the more shows off
> Your wonder: but yet speak; first you, my liege.
> Comes it not something near?
>
> (5.iii.21–3)

Her invitation to Leontes to respond resounds with a mischievous irony wholly in keeping with her earlier rebelliousness. One of the fundamental pleasures of romance as a genre is the pleasure elicited by surprise. In an eagerness to criticise romance for its lack of naturalism, surprise is quickly transmuted into coincidence. Shakespeare builds into this scene – into the time between the unveiling of the statue and its transformation into living woman – the opportunity to fully relish that pleasure. This skilful drawing out of the moment is very similar in technique to the reconciliation scene between Pericles and Marina in *Pericles*.

Leontes is so struck by the likeness, that he imagines the statue should scold him for not declaring it really is Hermione, but corrects himself by suggesting that in 'not chiding', the statue is most like Hermione since she was 'as tender / As infancy and grace' (ll. 26–7). When he remarks on the apparent age of the statue, something which is entirely credible because his last sight of his wife was 16 years ago, Polixenes offers a polite, courtly rebuttal, seeking to balance his friend's possibly rash artistic judgement in case Paulina is offended. Rather than being offended, Paulina acknowledges the accuracy of Leontes' comment because she is, of course, preparing to bring the statue to life. This provokes Leontes to study closely what he has lost, and his use of the word 'soul' (l. 34) reminds us instantly of his guilt, and the years he has spent in penitence, before he returns to commenting on the statue's 'natural posture', which clearly fascinates him. The antithesis in 'cold' and 'warm' (ll. 35–6) embellishes the established antithesis in alive and dead, and in Leontes' subsequent image we have a useful clue as to how this scene is intended to

progress dramatically. However amazed Leontes is – stunned to
silence at the beginning and stimulated by the statue's natural appearance to notice its age – he has yet to respond more deeply and
recognises this himself when he says:

> I am asham'd: does not the stone rebuke me
> For being more stone than it?
>
> (5.iii.37–8)

His mode of address is then clearly aimed at the statue itself, 'O royal
piece!' and his imagery stresses the magical nature of the experience
and helps make sense of Perdita's otherwise curious action in kneeling to the statue moments later.

Leontes differs from Pericles in one hugely significant way.
Whereas the worst Pericles can be accused of is overconfidence in
his wooing of Antiochus's daughter, Leontes' jealousy makes him far
more culpable and his sins have had to be paid for by his sustained
celibacy and daily act of penitence. It is important that at this
moment of reconciliation and restoration, he is honestly aware of
his culpability. To forget or ignore his guilt would be to doubly
punish Hermione, as Paulina herself recognises a little later in the
scene (5.iii.106–7). But it is not only Leontes who is swept up now in
this deeper, magical response. His words tell us that Perdita, too, is
affected. She stands, ironically, 'like stone' (l. 42) in admiration, her
'spirits' neutralised in wonder; but her immobility is only a metaphor,
and her rapt involvement in the words and actions of her father are
cleverly conveyed in the way she adds to his appeal: 'And give me
leave' (l. 42), as though she, also, were addressing her mother.

Admitting the strangeness of her desire to kneel and seek the
statue's 'blessing', Perdita nonetheless dismisses any idea of 'superstition' and in her carefully chosen terms of address, 'Lady, / Dear
queen' (ll. 44–5), it is intriguing to speculate on what religious
overtones these very Catholic words may have carried in a Protestant
theatre. The conflict over dogma and idolatry, which fuelled a lot of
anti-Catholic propaganda, meant that this entire scene, with its religious overtones and iconic statue, could not escape strong Christian
connotations in the audience's mind. In this case, Perdita's words

take on a specific Protestant meaning. In kneeling before the statue, she is openly denying before a Protestant audience, any Catholic trait or weakness. 'Superstition' was one of the commonest charges levelled at Catholics by Protestant rhetoricians. The apparent ease with which Shakespeare insinuates such clear Protestant ideology into stage worlds ruled by an eclectic crew of Greek and Roman gods is quite astonishing. It throws into sharp relief the whole business of metaphysics in his work. Put most crudely: who exactly are Apollo, Jupiter, Diana and the rest?

In an introductory study we have to satisfy ourselves with less challenging enquiries, and returning to Perdita, we can see from the rhythm which isolates the address 'Lady, / Dear queen', that she must indeed at least move to kneel at this point and appeal to the statue for its hand. Since Paulina tells her to kneel later (5. iii. 118), it is likely that she is prevented here. This interpretation is confirmed by Paulina's anxious warning about wet paint, which may even be accompanied by an action preventing the over-eager Perdita from touching her mother.

As Paulina's game continues, Camillo, Polixenes and Paulina all exhibit the same concern to allay Leontes' apparent suffering. Camillo uses the word 'sorrow', Polixenes 'grief' and Paulina the phrase 'Would thus have wrought you' (l. 58) to convey their desire to lessen Leontes' pain. Leontes and Perdita remain silently rapt because, as we have outlined, they have gone from surprise and wonder to a much deeper, emotional reaction, something beyond the comprehension of the others who do not belong to this family, whose blood is not stirred. Shakespeare fastens the dramatic focus rigidly on the husband and daughter.

Paulina appears to be so concerned that she moves to conceal the statue again, not once, but twice, prompting Leontes' abrupt demands, 'Do not draw the curtain' (l. 59) and 'Let be, let be!' (l. 61). The courtly etiquette that accompanied the original artistic tour has been dropped under the weight of emotion. Paulina's pleasure in controlling the situation is clear in her teasing remarks about the statue coming to life. The use of antithesis deepens when Paulina introduces the idea of motion. By threatening to take the statue from his sight, Paulina allows Leontes not only to voice his astonishment at the statue's verisimilitude in terms that focus on motion, but more importantly, to re-express his love for Hermione in terms which enhance the audience's anticipation of delight. When Paulina offers to 'afflict' him further, Leontes grasps at the word –

> For this affliction has a taste as sweet
> As any cordial comfort.
>
> （5.iii.76–7）

before he moves to kiss the statue. Once more Paulina intervenes to prevent her precious statue being touched. This time, her excuse that the paint is not yet dry becomes a metaphor itself for the manner in which she is managing this whole process. Her controlled, calm rhythm contrasts sharply with Leontes' urgent verse:

> The ruddiness upon her lip is wet;
> You'll mar it if you kiss it, stain your own
> With oily painting. Shall I draw the curtain?
>
> （5.iii.81–3）

When she wins from both Leontes and Perdita a joint desire to remain entranced, she is free to initiate the little drama she has engineered beforehand. What began as a simple visit to view a work of art has become something literally magical. For Jacobean audiences, magic was a reality, not a metaphor, and to reassure us of her good intent, Paulina insists that what she is doing is entirely free from evil influences. Her avowal wrings from Leontes a curiously worded agreement. The broken verse of his earlier speech gives way to a rigid, formal rhythm devoid of imagery but reverberating with sincerity. It has all the signs of a ceremonial statement, a public pronouncement or vow. In effect, it is Leontes' own arraignment. He places himself openly in Paulina's hands and sees through to its end the trust he placed in her on the day Apollo's oracle exposed his wickedness:

> What you can make her do,
> I am content to look on: what to speak,

I am content to hear; for 'tis as easy
To make her speak as move.
(5.iii.91–4)

The ceremonial, ritualistic nature of the proceedings is controlled by Paulina as she addresses all watchers, all audiences. Her request reaches beyond the world of Bohemia into the theatre itself, and she engages our susceptibility to romance as surely as she engages Leontes' eyes:

It is requir'd
You do awake your faith. Then all stand still:
Or – those that think it is unlawful business
I am about, let them depart.
(5.iii.94–7)

Leontes' answer, 'Proceed: / No foot shall stir' (ll. 97–8), has the same effect, reaching out into the theatre to silence the watchers and unite both audiences, real and stage, in wonder.

Paulina calls for music, the unnatural force which Shakespeare employs repeatedly when nature needs a little help in the late plays, with an abrupt, staccato list of imperatives, 'Music, awake her; strike!' (l. 98). As we have discovered, time has a pervasive influence in these plays, and we are reminded of Apollo's oracle as Paulina instructs the statue in another series of terse imperatives. But possibly the most intriguing question facing a director of the play is: when, precisely, does Hermione move? The rhythm and the sense all point to the same moment. Knowing that this resurrection will in effect 'fill' Hermione's grave, Paulina issues more precise commands, 'Stir, nay, come away' (l. 101), the sudden negative raising the spectre of failure but in so doing, keeping the illusion alive. The death/life antithesis is glaring, and there is an awareness of sound in her words that is itself striking. All this foregrounds the momentous half-line, 'You perceive she stirs' (l. 103).

Paulina's choice of the verb 'stir' is also informative, since in combination with her immediate instruction to Leontes and the rest, 'Start not' (l. 104), it evokes a tentative, shocking but slight movement, one that actually frightens the watchers. As Hermione now descends, Paulina reminds us there is nothing wicked about this business, and it does not require a great leap of contextual imagination to appreciate that her words might well have been a necessity in a Jacobean theatre, if the dramatisation was as effective and potent as I have been suggesting. That Leontes himself is frightened becomes clear from his movement away, allowing Paulina the opportunity to remind him yet again of his guilt:

> Do not shun her
> Until you see her die again; for then
> You kill her double.
> (5.iii.105–7)

But she possesses absolute control, and after a pause in which Hermione may have been allowed time to reach her husband, she kindly urges him to offer his hand to the vision. The repeated use of antithesis comes into its own again when Leontes exclaims 'O, she's warm!' (l. 109), while Camillo and Polixenes are given the chance not only to utter their surprise, but to tell us exactly what Hermione is doing: 'She embraces him!' (l. 111), 'She hangs about his neck!' (l. 112). It is valuable information, because however unreal our expectations of Shakespearean romance might be, its most potent actions are indelibly naturalistic.

Urged by Camillo and Polixenes to explain, Paulina employs a familiar Shakespearean ploy. She calls direct attention to the unreal nature of what has taken place, thereby reinforcing that reality, yet simultaneously urging us to consider the question of the relationship between appearance and reality far more deeply. After answering them, she appears to return all attention back to the embracing couple, and stresses the silent joy of their reconciliation. But Paulina has one further task to complete if she is to fulfil Apollo's oracle. She gently urges Perdita to 'interpose' (l. 118) – an oddly formal term unless she is being humorous, which is not as unlikely as it might at first sound. Throughout this whole performance, there has been an undercurrent of irony Paulina has evidently enjoyed, and a gently comical remark at this point is the perfect way to separate Leontes and Hermione. There is a crisp paradox in 'Our Perdita is found' (ll. 120–21), and in the same moment, the family we have seen torn asunder by jealousy is finally reborn. If the late plays are united in a romantic concern to evoke pleasure, that pleasure appears yet again to be inescapably rooted in what are perceived as the superior joys of family life, forgiveness and harmony.

5

The Tempest

Estrangement and Family Disruption

Two families are split apart in *The Tempest*, but the first split we experience, the division of Ferdinand and Alonso, is entirely secondary in the play as a whole. Alonso is driven to suicidal thoughts through grief, and Ferdinand voices his own grief too, but they are adjuncts to the central estrangement experienced by Prospero and Miranda. The work of explaining how this beautiful young girl and her irascible wizard father came to be on a lonely island is done early enough in the play but in a very plodding fashion. Coming immediately after the dramatic opening storm and shipwreck, Prospero's account of their history (1.ii.22–186) is a lengthy dialogue in which Miranda's part is merely to punctuate her father's speech. Romance time and again exerts its own peculiar pressure. Although, in this play, Shakespeare chooses the most challenging way to deal with the expansive nature of romance and opts to compress all the action into less than one day, nonetheless the heart of the play's meaning and interest lies in the exile and isolation of Prospero and his innocent daughter over the extended period it requires for her to reach nubility. Miranda is like Marina and Perdita in this respect, and only Imogen stands out as an adult woman.

In *Pericles* a storm, birth and death all take place simultaneously. In *Cymbeline* the forced, hasty parting of husband and wife occurs against the backdrop of their being discovered by her furious father. In *The Winter's Tale* the shocking public denunciation of an innocent queen for adultery, her arrest and the removal of her child, ravages the family unit. In *The Tempest*, however, the appalling destruction of normality and harmony is long past and in Act 1, Scene ii, Shakespeare uses Miranda's innocence as the means by which the story of their fall and exile can be retold. The audience, like Miranda, are ignorant of this history until Prospero tells his story.

To express her sense of pity at the tale Prospero tells, Miranda uses the type of remarkably direct, yet effective image common to the late plays, 'Your tale, sir, would cure deafness' (1.ii.106). In contrast is Prospero's reply, where he employs a complex metaphor:

> To have no screen between this part he play'd
> And him he play'd it for, he needs will be
> Absolute Milan.
>
> (1.ii.107–9)

The key image, 'screen', is richly ambiguous. It might refer to Prospero, who is screening Antonio from the real power he wants by retaining his title of Duke and only allowing Antonio a role as regent, Antonio wishing to remove that 'screen' and become sole ruler. But the possibility of a pun on 'play'd' where besides simply meaning 'stood in for' it can also describe Antonio's treachery, a game he is 'playing', implies it is Prospero who is being screened from the rest of the world, and consequently from Antonio's treachery, by his semi-retirement. It is a compressed and fertile image, and one that would hardly surprise us much on the lips of Macbeth or Hamlet. This contrast points once more to the extreme range of poetry to be found in the late plays, in spite of their dependence on romance sources.

Prospero recounts how Antonio's greed for power drove him to seek help from the King of Naples and in so doing betray the state itself before assisting an invading army into the city, then capturing Prospero and his infant daughter. Having opened this part of the story with the signpost, 'Now the condition' (l. 120), Prospero proceeds at some speed until he reaches the point in the story where they are both expelled. Here (1.ii.132) Miranda interrupts. Why? Prospero began to tell Miranda her history at line 36, and he concludes it 148 lines later. By any measure this is a substantial chunk of narrative unbroken by action, and without Miranda's interventions, it risks being dull indeed. Besides eliciting our sympathy, Miranda's words break this tale up into manageable chunks. Yet why then embark on such an unwieldy narrative at all? As already hinted at, we are in the world of romance sources. Although no single source has definitively been identified for *The Tempest*, the motif of the wizard nobleman and his daughter is ubiquitous in folk tale and romance literature. Essentially what Shakespeare faced when using it was the same dramatic problem he encountered repeatedly with all his romance sources, that is, how to compress the passage of time without sacrificing dramatic impact. In *The Tempest*, his solution is perhaps the most radical and risky of all, since he compresses the events of the play into a mere three or four hours. He could just as easily have begun his play with the machinations of Antonio in Milan, and the drama of their expulsion and abandonment at sea, which we can immediately see gives us a play much closer to *Pericles*. *Pericles* was without doubt written a few years before *The Tempest* and it is very tempting to see the aging dramatist improving on something with which he was not entirely satisfied.

Revealingly, it appears that Shakespeare was aware himself of the risk he was taking narrating the story via Prospero, as is evident in Prospero's own words:

> Hear a little further,
> And then I'll bring thee to the present business
> Which now's upon's; without the which, this story
> Were most impertinent.
>
> (1.ii.135–8)

Miranda then asks what is, as Prospero admits, a shrewdly sensible question: why were they not killed there and then? His answer reminds the audience that although they are dealing with a magician, his moral credentials are without question:

> Dear, they durst not,
> So dear the love my people bore me; nor set

A mark so bloody on the business; but
With colours fairer painted their foul ends.
(1.ii.140–3)

Hurried onto a ship, they were carried 'some leagues to sea' (l. 145)
and dumped into a 'rotten carcass of a butt' (l. 146) so unseaworthy
even the rats had left, all of which is pure fairy tale. Shakespeare has
until now restricted Prospero's narrative to a credible and naturalistic
explanation of the past. Here it slides smoothly and appropriately
(considering the role magic has to play in the linking of their story to
the shipwreck witnessed by Miranda) into the stuff of romance and
fantasy. Several images illustrate this shift into a style the literate
members of Shakespeare's audience would recognise particularly
from the love poetry of the period: 'th' sea that roar'd to us' (l. 149)
is complemented by 'th' winds, whose pity, sighing back again'
(l. 150), and the whole is wittily concluded with the paradoxical
'Did us but loving wrong' (l. 151).

This elevated tone continues when Prospero suggests Miranda was
sustained by strength from heaven, and in his description of his own
tears, 'When I have deck'd the sea with drops full salt' (l. 155), which
is equally reminiscent of love poetry of the period, where hyperbole
is almost inevitably the result of even mentioning tears. Prospero's
exaggeration does, however, have another side to it. He tells Miranda
that, far from being a burden, it was she who gave him courage and
strength. The same calm stoicism that thrills through Hermione,
reinvigorates Posthumus, and lifts Marina above the stench of the
brothel, maintained Prospero in his hour of most need. Although
their fall is the part of their history we have to imagine, Prospero and
Miranda, too, deserve and demand our sympathy.

Flight and Foreigners

Life on Prospero's isle may not closely match the foreign experiences
of Marina and Pericles in *Pericles*, or Posthumus in *Cymbeline*, but all
the shipwrecked characters in *The Tempest* recognise the oddity and
unreality of their new home and find their established relationships

threatened or unbalanced. Stephano and Trinculo fantasise about power and subjugate the gullible Caliban, while the lordly Alonso experiences a crippling impotence which renders him vulnerable to Antonio's murderous plotting.

A more foreign environment than that experienced by Ferdinand would be hard to find anywhere in Shakespeare. Like some Hamelin child, he is led onto the stage by the invisible, singing figure of Ariel to be confronted by Miranda and Prospero. What brings him there is music, and fortunately, versions of both Ariel's song here, 'Full Fathom Five', and his song from Act 5, Scene i, 'Where the Bee Sucks', exist in a collection printed in 1659. A detailed study of Elizabethan and Jacobean music is beyond the scope of this book, but the court music of the era was generally rather delicate, extremely harmonious and ordered. The lute was the favoured instrument to accompany songs, and the composer of these two songs, Robert Johnson, was a lutenist in the King's service after being apprenticed to the Lord Chamberlain, Sir George Carey, in 1596. It is also very apposite to appreciate that the educated minds of the period assigned great potency to music. In Shakespeare, music is used commonly to underpin celebrations of various kinds and provide an appropriate mood, as in the melancholy opening of *Twelfth Night* or Titania's lullaby in *A Midsummer Night's Dream*. In the late plays it is frequently used to accompany magic or as a curative. Music and dance were useful skills for an actor of the period and contemporary accounts suggest that the jigs, made especially famous by the comic actor Richard Tarlton, performed after plays, were hugely popular with audiences and some cause of concern to the City authorities.

So what takes place on stage here? Ferdinand's manner must demonstrate that he is being led by the same music that the audience can hear. That is, of course, a useful dramatic technique to draw the audience into the world of the characters, and in a play heavily dependent on magic and unreality, it is clearly more important to achieve this. This bemused state of mind is also reflected in Ferdinand's rather disjointed speech where he asks himself questions, and even corrects himself, 'thence I have follow'd it, / Or it hath drawn me rather' (1.ii.396–7). Ferdinand is also quick to attribute the music to a deity on the island, but his linking it to some supernatural cause is less curious if we accept his description of it, as well as the evidence of our own ears. Ferdinand believes it has physically calmed the storm and his sorrow. From the opening of the play the audience has witnessed Prospero demonstrating his magical power. Ferdinand is merely fitting into the established dramatic world: he knows he is in a wholly unfamiliar world, one in which the rules of reality may not apply.

The song itself mourns the loss of Ferdinand's father but its assumed knowledge of his fate, combined with the precious imagery and 'Sea-nymphs', also give it supernatural force, as Ferdinand observes when it ends. Additionally, Prospero's instructions to Miranda are highly formal and use a rather stately rhythm. Instead of 'Open your eyes and tell me what you see over there,' Prospero utters the wonderfully bombastic,

> The fringed curtains of thine eye advance,
> And say what thou seest yond.
>   (1.ii.411–12)

The reason is not hard to find and it is again to do with magic. Prospero frequently employs a rhythm, syntax and diction that exploit a shared cultural knowledge of spells, magicians and conjuration.

But there is also a potential difficulty here in terms of timing the action. Prospero's invisibility is not the issue. Shakespeare's audiences were not only well used to the convention that a character could simply be invisible on stage if he chose to be, but used to far more sophisticated conventions about space and the relationship of actors within that space. That Ferdinand doesn't see Prospero and Miranda here is not a problem. It is more of a problem to make Miranda not see Ferdinand until instructed to by her father. Earlier in the play, Prospero magically induces Miranda to sleep (1.ii.184–6) and that provides a clue as to what is happening here. If we are to make dramatic sense of Miranda's first sight of Ferdinand, it is likely that she must give an appearance of being similarly entranced, before opening her eyes and conveying all the wonder which goes with her words, 'What is 't? a spirit? / Lord, how it looks about!' (ll. 412–13).

That Shakespeare was concerned to create a dramatic *coup de foudre* is equally plain from the way Ferdinand speaks when he has seen Miranda: 'Most sure the goddess / On whom these airs attend!' (ll. 424–5). Yet precisely when Ferdinand sees Miranda is not at all clear either. Miranda has certainly had time and space enough to observe, praise and fall in love with Ferdinand while her father assures her that he is not a spirit but a mortal (ll. 412–24). But Ferdinand's stage behaviour is less obviously determined by his dialogue.

There is a clue in Prospero's aside, which informs the audience that the miraculous encounter of the two young people has been engineered by him. A director can choose to make the 'this' (l. 424) he refers to either just Miranda's awe, or the mutual attraction of the young couple. If the latter, then Ferdinand sees Miranda some time before he first speaks to her, and in his behaviour, too, he must convey sufficient awe and fascination to give rise to Prospero's gleeful aside. It is not an easy dramatic moment to bring to life effectively, but in the late plays realism is frequently sacrificed for more potent dramatic effects designed to exhibit very positive human behaviour and appeal to our emotions. This is a fine example. The immediate and naively eloquent way Miranda and Ferdinand fall in love is justifiably one of the play's most joyful moments.

That moment over, Ferdinand is quick to announce his own worth by referring rather obliquely to his royal blood. Prospero's tersely direct response prompts more speculation about what might take place on stage. Ferdinand's reply to Prospero's challenge is rich with possibilities. His opening image, 'A single thing' (l. 435), plays on ideas of his being alone, orphaned, lost, lonely, sincere and purposeful, but also reveals his quick intelligence, while the image of his tears in full flood adds credence to his grief. It is, of course, entirely fitting that he chooses an image from the sea to describe those tears. Given all this, we should not be surprised at all by Miranda's sympathetic interjection 'Alack, for mercy!' (l. 439). Ferdinand's words simultaneously prove him intelligent, noble and yet capable of feeling. Prospero himself has provided the clue to this earlier in the scene when describing Ferdinand to Miranda, 'but he's something stain'd / With grief (that's beauty's canker)' (ll. 417–18). We should also not be surprised that Ferdinand addresses himself to Miranda, because it is the attraction of the two young people that is driving the action. It is that which needs foregrounding above all else in any imaginative staging. The audience is, like Prospero in this scene, delighted voyeurs of youthful passion. So engrossed in Miranda is Ferdinand, that he has not really recognised Prospero's initial challenge for what it was. Prospero not only has to repeat himself to be heard across their interlocking gazes, 'A word, good sir; / I fear you have done yourself some wrong: a word' (ll. 445–6), but he also has to adopt an even more challenging tone since Miranda immediately says, 'Why speaks my father so ungently?' (l. 447).

Miranda also tries to impress, and her appeal on Ferdinand's behalf, combined with her disarmingly honest choice of words, 'This / Is the third man that e'er I saw; the first / That e'er I sigh'd for' (ll. 447–9), fuels his ardour even more. Not only is she a virgin (as he quickly acknowledges) but she loves him too. Again he ignores Prospero and instead addresses the beautiful vision in front of him. There is something comic in this whole business, where Prospero's gravity is drowned by the young couple's admiration. Prospero tries another challenge, which goes unheeded, and explains in an aside (ll. 453–5) his motives for interfering, but has to repeat himself yet again before finally succeeding in gaining the young man's attention. We may even see something magical in his imperative, 'I charge thee / That thou attend me' (ll. 455–6), an action of some kind, which at long last breaks Miranda's hold on Ferdinand. The substance of his accusation here, and the apparently unreasonable anger he exhibits, are also key features of the romance motif which is the source of the play, where the elderly magician demands that the young suitor perform some tasks before winning his daughter's hand.

Ferdinand's denial of any wrong is immediately supported by Miranda's more eloquent, but highly contemporary defence, 'There's nothing ill can dwell in such a temple' (l. 460). The Renaissance habit of linking physical and moral beauty finds its roots in Plato. Modern, less aesthetically aware audiences may find Miranda's idea charmingly naive, or even objectionable. Prospero sticks to his angry, imperative tone, and describes the punishment in store for Ferdinand in terms that owe as much to contemporary accounts of shipwrecked sailors as they do to fairy tale. This threat finally brings about a clear action and Ferdinand draws his sword.

This comic tussle between ardent youth and testy paternalism sees Ferdinand frozen in his defence while Miranda physically tries to make her father desist, 'Hence! hang not on my garments' (l. 477). When that fails, and his anger increases, Miranda resorts to honesty again to refute Prospero's attempts to undermine Ferdinand's physical appeal. 'To th' most of men this is a Caliban' (l. 483) is a crude lie, which Miranda's honesty neatly exposes, 'My affections / Are then most humble; I have no ambition / To see a goodlier man' (ll. 484–6).

Prospero's magic prevails and, amazed, Ferdinand describes for us his helplessness against both Prospero's and Miranda's very different charms. The weighty sources of his grief become light in the scales Miranda holds, and he finally expresses his surrender in terms that love poets of the period would readily comprehend. Love is a welcome prison, and liberty a price easily paid when the loved one becomes the entire world.

Magic has a reality in the world of *The Tempest* that is hard to access today. A failure to render the dream-like, dangerously unpredictable, foreign world of Prospero's island more palpable is a betrayal of the play itself. And as a final pointer in this direction, throughout this episode not only has Prospero spoken in asides to the audience, but he has also addressed Ariel in this way. Is Ariel present on the stage during this scene? And if so, how would we expect him to behave? How would Prospero himself communicate with him?

New Identities

Bewitched by Prospero, Ferdinand is later discovered enslaved, and carrying logs as Prospero promised. There are clear links between this episode and the discussion that introduces Florizel and Perdita to us in *The Winter's Tale*. In both cases, the two young lovers profess their love for each other against the threatening shadow of parental disapproval. Both Florizel and Ferdinand adopt lowly roles to court their lovers. In effect the only missing element which we might have come to expect is, in fact, disguise. In the case of *The Tempest*, the disapproving father is a willing witness to their intimacy.

Believing her father to be asleep, Miranda visits Ferdinand and finds him quite cheerfully engaged on the arduous task Prospero has set him. Strictly speaking, Miranda is disobeying Prospero by visiting Ferdinand in this secretive manner, but this rebellion is a necessary act if she is to achieve adulthood. In this respect Miranda resembles Imogen in *Cymbeline*, since they both confront their fathers over their choice of husband. Ferdinand, too, chooses independently of his father, something he apologises to Alonso for, later in the play (5.i.190–1). So although there may not be the same element of disguise in *The Tempest*, there certainly is the same adoption of the new, adult identities and roles which can lead to family reconciliation and regeneration.

What Miranda sees when she visits the young man her father has enslaved, and the audience must see too, is a Ferdinand busily and energetically engaged in the mundane task of moving logs from point A to point B. Her concern for him is self-evident in her request that he stop working and rest, but it is more eloquently conveyed in two images. The first, her wish that the lightning had destroyed the logs before he was asked to pile them up, and the more interesting, 'when this burns, / 'Twill weep for having wearied you' (3.i.18–19). The latter may initially appear unremarkable, but if we recall Perdita's eloquent use of language, something very similar is happening. The rhythm of the speech builds up to this image. It is made to stand out by a distinct pause before the final sentence about Prospero sleeping. The image relies on Miranda selecting out one log, either by hand or by eye, and then on our appreciating that wood can indeed 'weep', ooze resinous liquids, when it burns. It is a fine example of the kind of poetic conceit that dominates expression in the Renaissance period. The most inanimate of objects can be made to feel the most intense emotions in order to provoke sympathy for an unrequited lover. Miranda's use of it marks her out as both intelligent and sophisticated, yet simultaneously there is something utterly naive and guileless about it. She is so familiar with the sight of burning logs, leading the kind of life she does on this island, that the image springs naturally to mind. Rhythmically, her speech focuses our attention on the conceit, and it is a strong indicator of her character because she is using it to try and win sympathy not for herself, but for Ferdinand.

Ferdinand, however, is more concerned to behave as an independent, physically capable youth should do and dismisses outright any notion that he rest or that Miranda assist him, even when she physically tries to intervene, as she must do to make sense of 'pray give me that; / I'll carry it to the pile' (ll. 24–5). In his form of address, like Florizel, he displays a simple devotion that is entirely honourable and polite. It would 'dishonour' Miranda if he sat 'lazy by' while she worked. Miranda rejects his notion of honour as misguided since she would do the task much more willingly, but ironically she is wrong. The audience has already heard Ferdinand in his opening speech of this scene (ll. 1–14), say how happily he works knowing it is somehow for Miranda. However we may respond to Miranda's desire to assist Ferdinand, it is Prospero who guides us most pertinently. His choice of 'Poor worm' and 'infected' (l. 31) stresses Miranda's helpless weakness, making this relationship appear inevitable, however much he claims to control it.

When Miranda observes that he looks fatigued, Ferdinand denies it with a conventional compliment that assures us of his love while not elevating him above the object of his love, before asking Miranda her name in a manner that needs some explanation:

> I do beseech you, –
> Chiefly that I might set it in my prayers, –
> What is your name?
>
> (3.i.34–6)

Why would Ferdinand need to interrupt what is a straightforward question? What does the interruption itself tell us? We learned from *The Winter's Tale* how much stress was placed on Florizel's chaste love of Perdita. Shakespeare took some pains to avoid any implication that the two young lovers were in any way sexually involved. Chastity is something the heroines of the late plays maintain a ferocious grip on. He could easily have avoided this if he wished to, and where necessary, as in *Romeo and Juliet*, was perfectly able to stress the opposite. In *The Tempest* he takes great pains to protect Miranda's virginity, and so

Ferdinand interrupts his request for her name with the proviso that he only wishes to know so that he can use it in his prayers. It is a way of making sure we do not doubt the legitimacy of Ferdinand's love or suspect for a moment that he may be capable of deception. If we remember who he is, or more pertinently who his father is, we can see why that might be very desirable. Disarmed, Miranda is quick to reply and reveal comically that she has disobeyed her father to do so. Ferdinand is equally quick to toy with the name Shakespeare coined for her and to court her with exuberant praise.

But what follows presents us with some delicious food for thought since it appears to unbalance the essentially good character that Shakespeare has established for Ferdinand, and that we have just so clearly demonstrated. He admits that he has experience of other women and his choice of sensual imagery may even suggest an amusing degree of intimacy. A sexually experienced Ferdinand is an extremely uncomfortable partner for the quintessentially innocent Miranda, so how can we reconcile him with the chaste Ferdinand we have likened to Florizel?

After his eulogistic exclamations, Ferdinand makes a lengthy speech (3.i.39–48) about his attitude towards women. Enjambement gives it energy and fluency but it has a clear and definite structure that controls and defines its purpose, and that purpose is not to charac-terise Ferdinand at all. In the first of three stages, Ferdinand admits that 'many' women have impressed him with their beauty and 'many' have seduced his 'too diligent ear' (l. 42) with the quality of their voice or speech. What he wishes to concentrate on is the fact that his past has involved 'many' women, not what they were like or how varied they were, but that there were 'many'. That this is the case becomes even clearer in the second stage where 'many' is refined into 'several'. The compact balance of 'for several virtues / Have I lik'd several women' (ll. 42 –3) forms the heart of the whole sentence. It is also important that it is their 'virtues' Ferdinand was attracted to. The final step is to refine his history even further and build up to the true subject and purpose of the speech. He could not admire one of these women without noticing 'some defect' in her which ultimately undid her virtues. His climax deals wholly with the same subject that opened this speech, Miranda:

> but you, O you,
> So perfect and so peerless, are created
> Of every creature's best!
>
> (3.i.46–8)

The alliteration of 'perfect' and 'peerless' combines with the repetitious 'you' to produce a perfectly formed little eulogy on Miranda. The speech, then, is not at all about Ferdinand but about Miranda. Its entire purpose is to justify her name. And to do this, it must, of course, compare her with other women, and to the reality of relationships with those women.

Ferdinand has praised Miranda and declared his love: Miranda now does exactly the same, even in the same terms. She concludes her speech with specific information about tone, accusing herself of prattling. Even allowing for irony, this is as clear and obvious as we can expect from any dramatist. If we are seeking an imaginative staging, we have to take this into account, although not blindly or without also taking into account her own character. Taking her cue from Ferdinand's comparison of her with other women, Miranda initially reminds us just how innocent she is. The only female face she has ever seen is her own, in a mirror. The only men she has ever seen are Ferdinand, who she already refers to as 'good friend' (l. 51), and her father. That she has understood the theme of Ferdinand's speech, the comparison of her with the 'many' women he has known, is evident as she tells him that she has a complete ignorance of how people look elsewhere, to which she adds her own eloquently appropriate declaration of love, sealed with her own virginity.

On Prospero's island, her virginity is indeed her only dowry, but her effort to eulogise Ferdinand might strike us as weak compared with his fulsome effort. If we accept how strongly her speech is connected to his, how she has taken all her cues from his original theme of comparison, then it is entirely logical that she should finish by saying even her imagination could not create a form as attractive as his. Unlike Ferdinand, she has had nothing to draw comparisons with, except her imagination.

So to what extent is she justified in describing this as wild 'prattle'? Her speech is complex and quite sophisticated. She moves in logical steps from the idea of her own ignorance of women, to men, to people in general, and then to her declaration of love, which she enforces with as relevant a compliment as she could possibly make. Put another way, we might expect her wild 'prattle' to appear disjointed, rhythmically unpredictable or illogical, something more similar to Leontes' jealousy in *The Winter's Tale*. What is really happening when Miranda dismisses her speech as 'prattle' is further characterisation. It is her modesty that makes her try to rein in the excesses of her heart. The dutiful, obedient daughter is for the first time experiencing feelings which put a strain on that duty and obedience. She knows she has spoken with an overflowing heart, devoid of all rational duty, and tries to limit the damage. An actress taking the indicator, 'But I prattle / Something too wildly,' too literally would, in practice, find it a somewhat challenging task.

Ferdinand is bolstered by Miranda's words and announces his pedigree as a prelude to his proposal. After energetically defending his current 'slavery', he passionately expresses his love, yet via a religious image, 'Hear my soul speak' (l. 63). Miranda's direct and simple 'Do you love me?' (l. 67) allows him a second outburst of emotion in the form of a prayer before his emphatic list, 'Do love, prize, honour you' (3.i.71–3), which is itself graded to end with the essentially virtuous 'honour' when Miranda merely asked for 'love'. Her tears of joy move Prospero to speak and his interjection is again a clear guide for the audience. It is important that the irascible father begins to relinquish control, but Shakespeare makes him do so in especially significant terms.

As in the case of the love between Florizel and Perdita, the love between Miranda and Ferdinand is purged of even the faintest hint of lust or impropriety. It is central to Shakespeare's overall dramatic aim, the family reconciliation, that this is so, and therefore Prospero, the one figure most threatened by Ferdinand's interest in Miranda, also stresses their virtue:

> Fair encounter
> Of two most rare affections! Heavens rain grace
> On that which breeds between 'em!
>
> (3.i.74–6)

There is another clear indicator here not just of the tone of the dialogue, but of the entire scene. Like us, Prospero is a witness, and if he describes it as a 'Fair encounter / Of two most rare affections' (ll. 74–5), perhaps that is what it should be. Striving to make the scene too realistic, to place two adolescents on stage and let them interact, ignores the magical backdrop against which everything on the island takes place.

This explains why the remainder of the extract proceeds with the speed and simplicity elsewhere seen as a kind of dramatic shorthand. Asked why she is crying, Miranda's response is at first paradoxical and witty,

> At mine unworthiness, that dare not offer
> What I desire to give; and much less take
> What I shall die to want.
>
> (3.i.77–9)

but only to permit her to abandon all artifice for direct honesty and simplicity, 'But this is trifling' (l. 79), 'Hence, bashful cunning!' (l. 81). Framing her words in a prayer, like Ferdinand she finally declares her love in unequivocal terms, vowing to be his wife, maid or servant, or else die. The text is tantalisingly devoid of help as regard action here. Ferdinand perhaps kneels to underline his acceptance, although it is clear they take each other's hands before Miranda makes possibly the most abrupt exit in the entire Shakespeare canon. Yet even that abruptness makes dramatic sense since this whole encounter has been building up to their mutual declaration of love and intent to marry. Both have been tested by Prospero and have declared their love, one test of many which *The Tempest* exposes to our judgement, but certainly one very central to the late plays' overarching concern with family and regeneration. It is perhaps occasionally worth restating what may be obvious, and in these plays Shakespeare appears to regard pure love as an absolute requirement for family harmony and stability.

Trials and Tests

The banquet scene in *The Tempest* is especially perplexing because it demands an unusual amount of physical action unsupported by dialogue, and has some tantalisingly unclear stage directions to aid an imaginative staging. The stage direction early in Act 3, Scene iii, that describes the entrance of the spirits, may be unusually lengthy and detailed for Shakespeare as a whole, but is nonetheless tantalizingly vague. What are *'several Shapes'*, *'strange music'*, *'gentle actions of salutations'*? What precisely was the *'quaint device'* that Ariel employs to remove the banquet? Fortunately scholars have expended a lot of energy on some of these questions.

It is clear that some of the later plays were produced in the new indoor theatre at Blackfriars, as well as at the Globe, and it has been argued that the subtlety of some of the action in them suggests Shakespeare was consciously writing for a more intimate, indoor space. Similarly, these plays were given private court performances in state rooms which functioned only temporarily as theatres, so that for action which in the Globe may have involved complex stage machinery of some kind, such as a way of making Ariel fly, the company would have had to use something simpler. Music played a significant part in these plays, as it did in the increasingly popular court entertainment, masques. These also involved more scenery, props and expensive costumes, since lavish extravagance was part of the intended effect. It is difficult to overestimate the excess and luxury of the Jacobean court. We can be reasonably sure that some found its way onto the stage and that in *The Tempest*, Shakespeare was, at the very least, exploiting a taste for the exotic. It is there in the whole shipwreck motif, in the magic and in the Italianate characterisation and plot.

We can therefore be reasonably sure that the music, dance and 'living drollery' (3.iii.21) which so entrances the stage nobles was equally intended to entrance us. After witnessing it Sebastian says he will believe even the most unbelievable travellers' tales and Antonio agrees with him. The honest and entirely trustworthy Gonzalo remarks more appositely that though the creatures they have just seen had 'monstrous' shapes their behaviour was gentler and kinder than that of many civilised men. It is the cue for Prospero to condemn the other three as worse than 'devils', in an aside from his privileged station somewhere above the action, visible to the audience but conventionally invisible to the other characters. It may even be that his use of 'devils' is deliberately ironic and might point to the demonic appearance of some of the monstrous shapes. Certainly monstrosity and misshapenness were unnatural catastrophes readily associated in the contemporary mind with Satan.

On the other hand, Alonso praises their 'excellent dumb discourse' (l. 39) and is so struck by what he has witnessed that he believes it almost beyond rational contemplation. The venial Sebastian is quick to turn to more immediate concerns but out of courtly respect asks Alonso if he will eat first. Alonso is, however, still musing on what he has seen and, though hungry, dismisses the idea curtly. It is the honest Gonzalo who brings him out of his reverie and persuades him to eat, when he suggests that things they would never have believed as children have since become common knowledge. For the Jacobeans, lengthy sea journeys were still extremely dangerous adventures, rich with possibilities. Gonzalo draws his proof from the practice then in common use of leaving behind a substantial sum of money as a form of investment, which would be repaid fivefold if the traveller returned safely or with whatever he set out for. Alonso is convinced but approaches the banquet with anything but relish.

Under the cloud of his drowned son, Alonso appears to hope the banquet might indeed prove poisoned as life holds no pleasure for him, the best being past. The formality also allows all the characters present to approach the table to witness the 'quaint device' Shakespeare has in store for them as Ariel appears and magically removes the food, leaving them furious and hungry. Whether or not trapdoors were used, or a stagehand hidden beneath the table, really shouldn't cause much anxiety, as long as we recognise the necessity of making the removal of the banquet depend on both Ariel's visual action and some magical illusion. Ariel is the embodiment of Prospero's will and the abrupt removal of the food a deliberate act designed to provoke the nobles to exhibit their true natures. It is a test they all fail in drawing their swords.

Ariel sets Alonso, Sebastian and Antonio on the first step of their road to acknowledgement of their guilt by openly indicting them, 'You are three men of sin' (l. 53), and linking their current dilemma to their previous sinful acts. Before they draw their swords, Ariel makes a clear connection between the natural world and the working of fate. 'Destiny' has caused the sea to cast them ashore on an uninhabited island precisely because they are not fit to live with civilised men. The irony of their thinking of the island's spirits as monsters, when they are themselves unfit to live in decent society, is barbed.

One of those very rare, helpful moments where a scrap of dialogue gives us a precise indication of what action is required by the actors, follows:

> I have made you mad;
> And even with such-like valour men hang and drown
> Their proper selves.
>> [*Alon., Seb., etc., draw their swords.*]
>> (3.iii.58–60)

For Shakespeare's audience, suicide was much more a sin than a tragedy. It was also an issue very much on the minds of intellectuals coping with the strains of Catholic and Protestant intellectual warfare. Ariel here mocks their attempts at bravery as the weak, fraudulent courage a suicide might show. Calling them 'fools' (l. 60), he reminds them that he and the other spirits are merely agencies of Fate and their physical weapons are as ineffectual as though they used them against the wind or waves. He shifts from mockery to magical control, and once again his words are a precise clue to the characters' stage behaviour. Their swords become too weighty, 'massy' (l. 67), for them to hold them up, by which we understand that Prospero's magic renders them physically weak, but mentally alert enough to hear the core element of this bizarre little trial.

Ariel begins his sentencing with 'But remember, – / For that's my business to you' (ll. 68–9), to stress the significance of what follows. He then openly explains why, and by what means, they came to be on the island. For usurping Prospero, and leaving him and his daughter to the mercy of the seas, 'The powers, delaying, not forgetting' (l. 73), have used the same natural force, the sea, against them. It is perhaps advantageous to compare Prospero with Leontes here. Whereas

Leontes' act of hubris is instantaneously punished, Prospero takes on the powers of a god apparently without cost. Ariel uses three words to describe the divine force that has brought the nobles to the island, 'Destiny' (l. 53), 'Fate' (l. 61) and finally 'powers' (l. 73), to ward off any idea that Prospero is hubristic. Prospero himself explains clearly to Miranda the reason for this, soon after the opening shipwreck:

> Know thus far forth.
> By accident most strange, bountiful Fortune,
> (Now my dear lady) hath mine enemies
> Brought to this shore; and by my prescience
> I find my zenith doth depend upon
> A most auspicious star, whose influence
> If now I court not, but omit, my fortunes
> Will ever after droop.
>
> (1.ii.177–84)

The Jacobeans had a deep-rooted fascination with astrology and in *The Tempest* Shakespeare makes it clear that Prospero is himself an agent of Fate. In the speech he makes to Miranda he stresses that it is in effect his duty to seize this opportunity, while his personal star shines most auspiciously.

Having named their crime, Ariel moves to their punishment via a very condensed, difficult piece of verse. Not only have the Fates taken Alonso's son, but they 'pronounce by me' (3.iii.76) that 'Ling'ring perdition – worse than any death' (l. 77) 'shall step by step attend / You and your ways' (ll. 78–9). Eternal damnation is a dreadful sentence indeed for a Jacobean audience, unshakeably Christian in outlook. But Ariel offers Alonso hope in his final few words, as in Christian terms he is bound to do. Either he endures a living damnation on the island, or he gains forgiveness by penitence, 'heart-sorrow' (l. 81), and by leading a blameless 'clear' (l. 82) life from now on. With that he vanishes as quaintly as he appeared, and the spirits return, we presume, to carry out a very practical bit of set changing as much as to taunt the still impotent nobles further.

It is clear that this curious episode in the play functions as an informal judicial trial, as well as a test, and sets the guilty on the road to penitence and ultimately reconciliation. Prospero uses Ariel as arresting officer, prosecutor, judge and jury, but having already imprisoned the defendants on the island, relies on time and their own consciences to bring about repentance. Once again we can see how strongly this locates the play within the literature of romance, where the human spirit is severely tested and the individual's potential for remorse deeply probed.

Time and Tide

After the dramatic opening scene aboard ship in *The Tempest*, Miranda speaks from the safety of dry land and pleads with her father to calm the storm:

> If by your Art, my dearest father, you have
> Put the wild waters in this roar, allay them.
> (1.ii.1–2)

The opening sentence is as neat a piece of dramatic exposition as any in Shakespeare. Not only is this strangely cloaked man a magician, but he is also the young girl's father. What reason he might have for creating this storm becomes of immediate interest as Shakespeare gives Miranda the vivid description necessary in a theatre empty of naturalistic effects. That description is often troublesome to modern audiences less tied to seasonal rhythms or used to such sights. To convey the deep blackness of the sky Miranda chooses the word 'pitch', a substance not only foul-smelling, but conventionally associated with sailors and sailing. Imagining the sky in the act of pouring the evil-smelling liquid earthwards, Miranda says the sea itself is so stormy it meets the sky, and extinguishes the fire, or lightning. In both *Pericles* (3.i) and *The Winter's Tale* (3.iii) there are strikingly similar descriptions of storms that rely essentially on the visual image of the line between the sea and the sky becoming confused by darkness and chaos, a profoundly cataclysmic vision.

Miranda sympathises with the poor sailors she imagines aboard the wrecked ship. Her essential kindness strikes us as she speaks of the sound moving her own heart, and of her wish that she had had the power of a god to prevent the disaster. Her whole speech is full of strong, imaginative images which reveal her 'piteous heart' (1.ii.14), and her state of distress is clear not just from the agitation of her own words, but from Prospero's measured attempt to calm her. So perturbed is Miranda that Prospero has to repeat his assertion that no harm has been done, and Shakespeare uses the opportunity to reinforce the fact that this is a father and a daughter, skilfully building the air of mystery by giving Prospero a speech so overtly enigmatic that it demands immediate explanation. He tells us that not only is Miranda ignorant of who she is, but she does not know her own father's identity or place of origin. If this were not strange enough, Miranda seems entirely unsurprised. The appropriateness of the moment is now given great weight by Prospero's single, ominous statement:

> 'Tis time
> I should inform thee farther.
> (1.ii.22–3)

while his taking off his magic garment, laying it and the storm aside, and his telling Miranda to be seated, all act as conventional signals that a narrative is to follow.

Having assured her that no one on the ship has suffered in any way, and consequently confused us, as we have witnessed their distress, Prospero begins his account of their past, again making clear that it is the proper time. However, Shakespeare has far too firm a grasp of fundamental dramatic technique to allow such an opportunity for suspense to go unexploited, and Miranda's confident assertion that she does recall some of her former life delays Prospero just enough to tease the audience. When it becomes clear she can only remember the faintest of images, Prospero reveals his identity as Duke of Milan and the audience finds itself on familiar ground with Miranda as she exclaims,

> O the heavens!
> What foul play had we, that we came from thence?
> Or blessed was't we did?
>
> (1.ii.59–61)

Anxious for the trouble she must have caused him in the past, Miranda is nonetheless now eager to hear more of their past and urges her father on. One of the characteristics Prospero displays is a tendency to digress, often indicated by his failing to finish sentences, which he does the moment he starts to tell of Antonio's treachery. As though aware, himself, of his own rambling style, Prospero even interrupts himself to see if Miranda is attending, but manages to fully recount Antonio's corruption with some degree of sophistication. Having first learnt how to advance and suppress suitors, and which over-ambitious individuals to check, he reshaped the loyalties of Prospero's former courtiers. Possessed of both the office and the effective exercise of power, Antonio steered the entire court against Prospero and in a final parasitic image, becomes

> The ivy which had hid my princely trunk,
> And suck'd my verdure out on 't.
>
> (1.ii.86–7)

In this first half of his narrative, we see Prospero showing a mystical awareness of the role time has played in his and Miranda's life so far. Unlike the other plays, *The Tempest* has an ambiguous attitude towards time. On one hand Prospero clearly exercises power over the very elements themselves and can exercise godlike power over the ship and those on board, yet he has also been forced by some greater power to await this particular moment, and reveals an acute sense of having to exploit these events as they are given him:

> and by my prescience
> I find my zenith doth depend upon
> A most auspicious star, whose influence
> If now I court not, but omit, my fortunes
> Will ever after droop.
>
> (1.ii.180–4)

But as with Pericles and Leontes, the most significant factor determining what part time plays in Prospero's life is the coming of age of his daughter. Only then can the estranged family be revived. The terrible actions that have destroyed the family, and the suffering inflicted on them, can never be undone. Time fosters forgiveness and repentance, and without them Leontes, Pericles and Prospero are slaves to anger, bitterness and pain. The families of the late plays are never truly restored, only revived. The requirement for a dowry and the normality of the extended family mean that it is simply an impossibility for the daughter to achieve any kind of marital happiness or success without being restored to her father in order that she may marry.

Suffering and Forgiveness

Early in Act 5, Prospero begins to draw all the various threads under his command into one pattern. The last the audience saw of Alonso, Sebastian, Antonio and the rest, was their panic and distraction brought on by the words and magical torments of Ariel at the end of Act 3. The good and guiltless Gonzalo described their state of mind then through a central image:

> All three of them are desperate: their great guilt,
> Like poison given to work a great time after,
> Now 'gins to bite the spirits.
>
> (3.iii.104–6)

Their role in Prospero's usurpation and his abandonment at sea with a baby daughter, Miranda, has been exposed by Ariel. Gonzalo's image is wonderfully apt and reinforces the view of suffering and forgiveness developed throughout this study. Guilt has worked on them 'Like poison' because of its delayed action. Time has been a necessary part of their experience, both of guilt, and of repentance. Alonso, as the central figure in the plot against Prospero, rushed off stage seeking to join his dead son 'i' th' ooze'. Like Posthumus, Alonso is driven to consider suicide, although unlike him, there is no thought of saving another through his own death. Grief and guilt combined push Alonso to the brink of life.

By the time we see the guilty company again at the start of Act 5, Ariel has kept the group intact, but the three sinners, Alonso, Sebastian and Antonio, are in a state which equates to punishment. Ariel tells Prospero that if he were to see them, he would feel sympathy for them, and Prospero, touched by the idea that a spirit 'which art but air' (5.i.21) can feel something of pity, orders Ariel to release them. The reason he gives is once more instructive.

> the rarer action is
> In virtue than in vengeance: they being penitent,
> The sole drift of my purpose doth extend
> Not a frown further.
>
> (5.i.27–30)

The decision Prospero makes to release them depends on their penitence. It is clear that all his actions in causing the shipwreck, separating Ferdinand and taunting the castaways with his magic, have been to bring them to an understanding of their own guilt and a state of true penitence. But unlike Alonso, whose suicidal urge we have already noted, the other two give no verbal or other indication of their being penitent at all. In fact when Sebastian and Antonio exit at the same time as Alonso, they do so with murderous, not suicidal intent, as during the course of their time on the island, Antonio and Sebastian plot together to murder Alonso, and are only prevented by Ariel (2.i.194–292), behaviour that suggests seasoned evil rather than penitence. How are we to resolve this apparent contradiction?

We can start by reminding ourselves that we are dealing with theatrical scripts for performance. As the lords enter, led by Ariel, their physical manner and action are significant before they ever speak. Alonso is given '*a frantic gesture*' which the others perform '*in like manner*'. Prospero provides us with a curiously useful image to accompany these gestures. He calls for music, the conventional therapy:

A solemn air, and the best comforter
To an unsettled fancy, cure thy brains,
Now useless, boil'd within thy skull!
(5.i.58–60)

The picture created is one of insanity, the lords half-crazed, distracted, their bodies shells devoid of reason or sense. The Renaissance mind was not inclined to sympathise with the lunatic. A figure
of fun and laughter, less than human, he is frequently used simply as
cheap entertainment in the works of other Jacobean playwrights.
What we need to envisage is the complete powerlessness and immobility of the troupe once they '*stand charm'd*' in Prospero's magic
circle, 'For you are spell-stopp'd' (5.i.61). For this brief moment,
the spellbound noblemen are dehumanised, reduced to their antithesis, something that moves Prospero to praise the one good man
amongst them.

Slowly, 'as the morning steals upon the night, / Melting the
darkness' (5.i.65–6), the spell begins to wear off and the noblemen
gradually assume full consciousness. Prospero again refers to their
loss of reason before cataloguing their misdeeds one by one. The
only guiltless one is dealt with first and Prospero acknowledges
Gonzalo's entirely trustworthy treatment of both himself, and
Alonso, by vowing to reward him 'both in word and deed', which
suggests a public declaration as well as a personal gain. Alonso is
next, but Prospero goes only as far as to accuse him of cruelty to
himself and Miranda before hastily moving on to Sebastian:

Thy brother was a furtherer in the act.
Thou art pinch'd for 't now, Sebastian.
(5.i.73–4)

That 'pinch'd' is vital, since whether or not it is intended to convey
both mental and physical hardship, it undoubtedly conveys the idea
of punishment. It recalls the threats that quelled his rebellious slave
Caliban, and is evident in the way Prospero then catalogues Antonio's faults. His crimes are seen as the most severe. He 'Expell'd
remorse and nature' (l. 76) to turn unnaturally on his own brother

and baby daughter. The 'Unnatural' reinforces the primacy of blood and family to be encountered repeatedly in these plays. Alonso may be wicked, Sebastian also, but Antonio's crime is the fundamental crime which unites Athenian and Jacobean audiences alike in horror, quite independent of any Biblical allusion to Cain and Abel. It is the crime that undermines the very foundation of a civilised society, so his 'inward pinches therefor are most strong' (l. 77), his guilt the most penetrating, his punishment the most severe. Knowing this, Prospero is still able to fulfil his promise at the opening of the scene, and say 'I do forgive thee' (l. 78).

The catalogue over, he now turns to the kind of overt description which pulses through Shakespearean drama like some essential fluid. Although the actors may be more than able to convey their slowly growing consciousness, Shakespeare appears more comfortable with the security of his own poetry and so Prospero once more resorts to the sea imagery that ripples through the entire play, to describe their gradual recovery. Finally, although having reached consciousness they still fail to recognise or even perceive him, Prospero instructs Ariel to dress him in clothes that will identify him as 'sometime Milan' (l. 86).

After years of banishment, loneliness and survival, Prospero's magic has brought together the three individuals who placed him in such a position, and driven them to the edge of madness. He has had the considerable pleasure of seeing two of them turn on the third, and yet been able to prevent further evil. His suffering ends where theirs begins.

Modern audiences find the lack of apparent contrition in Sebastian and Antonio worrying, and certainly, when this play is compared with *Cymbeline*, Shakespeare displays a notable lack of dexterity handling loose ends in *The Tempest*. Occasionally, it is worth plundering one great writer to enhance our understanding of another, and in *Middlemarch*, George Eliot offers this brilliant insight into the nature of guilt and the past: 'With memory set smarting like a reopened wound, a man's past is not simply a dead history, an outworn preparation of the present: it is not a repented error shaken loose from the life: it is a still quivering part of himself, bringing shudders and bitter flavours and the tingling of merited shame' (*Middlemarch*, chapter 61). This is a description that Shakespeare's audience (for whom disbelief in God was simply not a serious option) would have understood with great ease. More pertinently, it is one Antonio and Sebastian would have wilted under.

Divine Magic

From the dramatic storm and shipwreck that opens the play, to the humiliation of Stephano, Trinculo and Caliban that closes it, magic is ubiquitous in *The Tempest*. In the other late plays magic underpins dramatic moments of transformation, but here it pervades the whole, generating considerable critical speculation about the play's role in the Shakespeare canon because of a commonplace analogy between drama and magic driving much of the thinking that sees *The Tempest* as Shakespeare's swan song.

Shortly after narrating the history of their exile to Miranda, Prospero brings onto the stage the profoundly antithetical figures of Ariel and Caliban. He summons Ariel deliberately, and Ariel, in his first words, betrays a powerful affinity with nature:

> be 't to fly,
> To swim, to dive into the fire, to ride
> On the curl'd clouds.
>   (1.ii.190–3)

In describing the shipwreck Ariel's entire emphasis is on his control of the ferocious natural forces which drove all the nobles to throw themselves overboard in terror, forcing Ferdinand to proclaim, '"Hell is empty, / And all the devils are here"' (ll. 213–14). The paradox is glaring but only troublesome on the printed page. At this early stage in the drama we are still uncertain about who Prospero is and what his motives are. Miranda has voiced that concern for us and it is only when Prospero makes Ariel confirm that not a single life has been lost, that we begin to regard Prospero as virtuous. Ariel even provides the faintly comic assurance that, far from being harmed, the nobles have in effect had their clothes cleaned for them, a detail

Anne Barton makes ingenious use of in her essay, ' "*Enter Mariners wet*": Realism in Shakespeare's Last Plays' (*Essays, Mainly Shakespearean*, Cambridge University Press, 1994).

Though Ariel's name itself is indicative of his role and spiritual nature, he isn't without a will of his own and is soon in dispute with Prospero about his freedom. That quarrel permits Prospero to recount vital information about the island and the part magic plays in it. We learn that Prospero has released Ariel from some 'torment', and in anger he calls Ariel a liar and 'malignant', finally asserting his authority over the conventionally rebellious demonic servant by threatening to outdo the punishment inflicted by Sycorax, Prospero's 'oak' (l. 294) being naturally stronger than Sycorax's 'cloven pine' (l. 277).

Yet Prospero's tale of Sycorax has at least as much to do with the nature of his own magic as it does with Ariel's moodiness. In Sycorax, Shakespeare creates Prospero's antithesis. While his exile was the result of his own negligence, hers was a punishment for evil. The only reason the people of Argier did not execute her was because she was pregnant, 'for one thing she did / They would not take her life' (ll. 266–7). We learn that for failing to serve the evil witch Sycorax, and 'act her earthy and abhorr'd commands' (l. 273), Ariel was confined within a pine tree for twelve years, during which time Sycorax died, and only Prospero's mercy and magic freed him. Ariel's opposition to Sycorax's 'earthy' wickedness confirms his own higher spirituality, and underscores his new master's virtue. Shakespeare develops a deliberate antithesis in which the 'hag' Sycorax represents an earthbound, venial, self-gratifying use of magic while Prospero's art always partakes of the divine and has its eyes and purpose on heaven. Prospero, although intriguingly similar to Marlowe's Faustus, is unlike him in a highly significant way. Empowered by Satan, Faustus can only employ his great power on trivialities, to satisfy lust or make fun of the Pope. Empowered by heaven, Prospero seeks only greater knowledge of God, and earthly justice.

Prospero's depiction of the island as he found it is equally informative. With Sycorax dead, and Ariel imprisoned, it is a barbaric place, the only creature inhabiting it, Caliban, not meriting the term 'human'. In Prospero's view, Caliban is a 'whelp' (l. 283), his birth like that of a dog and his mother a witch, 'damn'd' (l. 263) beyond redemption. The contrast he draws between Ariel and Caliban is a potent reminder to the former of where his duty lies, and Ariel is quickly brought back into line. Prospero's authority is tempered by mercy and he promises Ariel his freedom in two more days, conditional on his performing Prospero's will till then.

Before Caliban appears, to make the contrast between good and evil magic more manifest, Prospero awakens Miranda so that her presence and behaviour can bolster this defining contrast. At the mention of Caliban's name, Miranda recoils, ' 'Tis a villain, sir, / I do not love to look on' (ll. 311–12). In calling for him Prospero repeats the earth–air antithesis by referring to him as 'Thou earth' (l. 316) and in denouncing him as the devil's son. Such remarks are critical guides when it comes to issues of design and staging, and to realise *The Tempest* with a Caliban untouched by these terrible stains is flying wildly in the face of the text. To suggest that the product of sinful lust between a witch and a demon could be physically undamaged or even sympathetic is a shocking misunderstanding of Jacobean metaphysics. Caliban is a monster, a word Stephano and Trinculo use (2.ii) without a hint of irony when they first encounter him.

Yet moments before he does appear, Ariel makes a bizarre and fleeting re-entrance disguised as a water nymph as Prospero instructed, merely for Prospero to whisper instructions in his ear and exit. This curious interruption might owe something to the fashion for masques and represent a good opportunity for a spectacular quick change, but it is far more likely that Shakespeare brings Ariel back, right into the midst of Prospero's yelling for Caliban, to reinforce the central antithesis around which all of Prospero's actions have to be interpreted. Against the glorious beauty of Ariel, how much more brutish must Caliban appear.

Caliban's first action is to curse, and his second, to complain. In both he reveals his corrupt nature by employing the language of witchcraft learnt from his mother. In the face of this, critical attempts to redeem him and render him sympathetic are commonplace. They are often based on crediting his account of his relationship with

Prospero, how the latter beguiled him into a profound metamor-
phosis, from king to slave, on his own island. Certainly his account
and Prospero's agree on two things: that his freedom has been
drastically curtailed and that his function is that of a slave. But to
regard this as in any way akin to the romantic motif of the bewitched
prince flies in the face of Prospero's precisely worded denial. 'Thou
most lying slave' (l. 346), Prospero says, in immediate response to
Caliban's tale of mistreatment and deceit, before claiming to have
treated Caliban with 'human care' (l. 348) within his own lodging,
until he attempted to rape Miranda.

There are no textual grounds whatsoever to dispute Prospero's
account. Caliban is indeed a liar and he did indeed attempt to rape
Miranda, as he himself admits gleefully, imagining how he might have
populated the entire island with little Calibans. It is his admission,
voiced in terms that contain not a shred of regret, which goads
Miranda herself to speak, and condemn him as an 'Abhorred slave'
(l. 353) not only incapable of good, but so quintessentially evil as to
be a danger to those good natures he encounters. In her mind, his
crime deserved far more than mere imprisonment.

It is all too easy from a modern perspective to empathise with the
downtrodden slave, the deformed victim of Mother Nature, as
though Caliban is somehow not the product of evil fertilising evil.
In the Jacobean mind he is evil personified: malformed, ignorant,
venial, selfish, lustful and above all, a terrible threat to innocence.
Like Lysimachus, Boult and Cloten, in attempting rape he threatens
to undermine the whole basis of civilised stability, familial love and
joy. For Miranda rape is a crime beyond forgiveness because it is the
only crime that denies the existence of love yet generates new life. No
wonder Caliban is called 'Hag-seed' (l. 367), 'malice' (l. 369), 'savage'
(l. 357), 'vile' (l. 360) and a number of other superlatively vicious
epithets.

Confronted with their united loathing, Caliban submits, but only
because of the fear of punishment carried in Prospero's threats. The
rather quaint aches and pains his master threatens to inflict on him
are clearly something Caliban has endured before, and he is held in
check only through the power of Prospero's divinely inspired magic,
which, Caliban admits,

is of such pow'r,
It would control my dam's god, Setebos,
And make a vassal of him.
                              (1.ii.374–6)

Revived Families

In *The Tempest*, the revival of a family again provides the dramatic
ending although in this case, there is quite a lot more which occurs on
stage before the curtain finally falls. With Ariel's assistance, Prospero
brings Alonso's party together and reveals himself to them. Alonso
has been so wrought upon by the magic of the isle and loss of
Ferdinand, that he instantly resigns his dukedom to Prospero and
admits his sin. The grave business of guilt and forgiveness over, the
play's tone changes almost instantly, as Alonso asks Prospero when
he lost his daughter. Prospero's brief, ironic, 'In this last tempest'
(5.i.153) may amuse the audience but cheats Alonso of any further
information, and Prospero turns instead to the amazed expressions
on the faces of the other lords. There is something amusing in his
choice of imagery to describe their shock but it is difficult to be
confident about how the particular images are intended to work.
Prospero's 'they devour their reason' (l. 155) may derive from the
conventional open-mouthed expression, but it is certainly putting the
language under some degree of strain if this is the case. This image is
closely followed by 'their words / Are natural breath' (ll. 156–7),
which suggests they are mute, their words transformed to breath,
which is entirely in harmony with the state of wonder Prospero wants
us to imagine when he uses the word 'admire' (l. 154). In this case,
'devour their reason' implies something more akin to being struck
dumb than to merely standing open mouthed. Reason is fruitless
without speech, and this view gains ground a little further on where
we find, 'howsoe'er you have / Been justled from your senses' (ll.
157–8), reinforcing the picture of them standing mute and impotent
with astonishment. To wholly remove any doubt, Prospero adds a
formal declaration of his title, history and present status until the
familiar caesura signals change, and he shifts from a formal, lordly

tone to a more amiable, relaxed one, suiting the disclosure he has in mind.

We began by suggesting there might be something amusing in Prospero's depiction of the astonished lords, and there is undoubtedly nothing grand or pompous in his description of his dwelling. Equally, his disclosure is anticipated by a generous repayment for the return of his dukedom:

> My dukedom since you have given me again,
> I will requite you with as good a thing;
> At least bring forth a wonder, to content ye
> As much as me my dukedom.
>
> (5.i.168–71)

His choice of 'wonder' plays on Miranda's name, but clearly also refers to the fact that Ferdinand is alive, a fact that must be in his mind when he formulates the link between his own pleasure at recovering his dukedom and Alonso's promised pleasure. It would be easy here to overlook the profundity of his comparison. In Prospero's balance, the family sits weightily in the scale against an entire dukedom.

In terms of staging, it must be the case that the discovery by Alonso of Miranda and Ferdinand *'playing at chess'* (5.i.171) is for the audience's eyes too. Their brief exchange before realising they are being observed, maximises the delight of the moment for Alonso, while allowing us the additional voyeuristic pleasure of their intimacy. Chess was remarkable in the period, in that it was considered an entirely suitable activity for two young people of the opposite sex to practise in private. Games of chess figure prominently in Jacobean drama as a device to bring young men and women together privately, and as a metaphor for the conflicts of courtship. Add to this the significance of virginity in these plays, and of Prospero's warning to Ferdinand in this respect, and it would be foolish for any production to introduce an element of sexuality into this temptingly voyeuristic moment. What the young couple actually say to each other may be irritatingly tainted with difficulty

over the precise meaning of 'wrangle', but the general aura of young
love's see-sawing between insecure complaint and denial, is easily
accessible.

Alonso is moved to speak first, as the focal point of this reconciliation, and his heartfelt anxiety that this may just be another trick of
the island is as eloquent as Ferdinand's response:

> Though the sea's threaten, they are merciful;
> I have curs'd them without cause.
>
> (5.i.178–9)

Between these personal expressions, Sebastian's public claim that this
is miraculous reverberates clearly, signifying his change of heart.
After all, he was largely goaded into contemplating evil by the already
corrupt Antonio.

Few words are expended on Alonso's and Ferdinand's reconciliation. The joyful father invites his son to embrace him, while the son
remains silent, for it is the reaction of Miranda that compels us. Her
awe parallels the earlier astonishment of the lords, but excitement
makes her as voluble as they were mute:

> O, wonder!
> How many goodly creatures are there here!
> How beauteous mankind is! O brave new world,
> That has such people in 't!
>
> (5.i.181–4)

Her short sentences almost stumble over each other with excitement,
which makes them appear purely for her own consumption, and
indeed she is not in any meaningful sense in a dialogue here with
any of the characters. Consequently it is her father who responds,
with the mild riposte, ''Tis new to thee' (l. 184).

Alonso's question to Ferdinand about Miranda's identity refers
superficially to the game of chess, while his shock at the brevity
of their acquaintance reminds us that the 'play' has adhered to the
classical unity of time. The paradoxical imagery he employs to express
his continued bewilderment is rich in possibilities:

> Is she the goddess that hath sever'd us,
> And brought us thus together?
>
> (5.i.187–8)

On one level he is still aware of being wholly at the mercy of the gods
on this island. Events have demonstrated this to him clearly enough.
Yet Ferdinand's falling in love with Miranda has indeed 'sever'd'
father and son in the sense of his having gained, via that choice,
independent adulthood. Ferdinand acknowledges this himself when
he replies by pointing out that he believed his father to be dead when
he chose Miranda. But the severing is only part of the story since
in wedding Miranda, Ferdinand was unwittingly reuniting his own
family, *and* the states of Naples and Milan, irony not wasted on the
diplomatic Gonzalo.

All of which foregrounds the earlier question: whose family is
being restored here? Clearly the dramatic focus is on Alonso's
reconciliation with Ferdinand, yet Prospero's reconciliation with his
own brother is evidently more than a mere side effect since so much
is made of the unification of the two states that results from Ferdinand and Miranda's marriage. In earlier plays we saw the single family
unit divided and restored. In *The Tempest* the potency of that single
family unit is extended until it becomes a metaphor for the state
itself, a feature of the play that unites it closely with *Cymbeline*. This
new coherence is stressed by Ferdinand when he answers Alonso's
question:

> She
> Is daughter to this famous Duke of Milan,
> Of whom so often have I heard renown,
> But never saw before; of whom I have
> Receiv'd a second life; and second father
> This lady makes him to me.
>
> (5.i.191–6)

We can see the same emphasis on this strengthened family in
Alonso's acceptance of a reciprocally paternal role, 'I am hers'
(l. 196), that allows him the penitent sincerity:

But, O, how oddly will it sound that I
Must ask my child forgiveness!
(5.i.197–8)

It is Miranda he is referring to. The sin, Alonso has already acknow-
ledged, and so Prospero saves him further suffering in terms that
dramatically unite *The Tempest* with the other late plays:

There, sir, stop:
Let us not burthen our remembrance' with
A heaviness that's gone.
(5.i.198–200)

This not only contains the vital forgiveness necessary on Prospero's
part for the new family to take shape, but also signals the larger
world's joyful acceptance of the new order:

I have inly wept,
Or should have spoke ere this. Look down, you gods,
And on this couple drop a blessed crown!
For it is you that have chalk'd forth the way
Which brought us hither.
(5.i.200–4)

For the faithful and unshakeably honest Gonzalo, only the gods
could have brought about such wonders and his divinely respectful
diction introduces a spiritual tone that now proceeds to dominate the
dialogue. Alonso affirms 'Amen' while Gonzalo draws together all
the strands of familial and state interest that have been leading to this
knot. His reference to 'gold on lasting pillars' (l. 208) conveys a
prospect of permanence while his repeated use of antithesis generates
finality.

As the perpetrator of wrong and originator of evil in the play, it is
Alonso who now concludes this private restoration with a public
gesture and wish that underline the source of corruption in the play,
envy:

Give me your hands:
Let grief and sorrow still embrace his heart
That doth not wish you joy!

(5.i.213–15)

Gonzalo maintains his hieratic role with 'Be it so! Amen!' and brings this reconciliation to a close before the entrance of Ariel introduces more unfinished business. What is perhaps most interesting is the way in which fairy tale and religion combine. It is clearly visible in Alonso's wish for the young couple and in Gonzalo's celebratory tone and religious diction throughout. It is an aspect of all the late plays that deserves deeper consideration. There is a potent mixture at work in which folk motifs and the enigmatic world of magic are tinged with an aura of spirituality rooted in both Christian and classical theology. In the late plays Shakespeare clearly probes some of his audiences' most sensitive beliefs, the metaphysical and the superstitious, in order to dramatically stimulate emotional responses to perhaps the most fundamental human experience of all, the family, its disruption and its reconciliation.

Further Reading

Texts

The editions of the late plays referred to in this book are all in the Arden series:

Cymbeline, The Arden Shakespeare, ed. J. M. Nosworthy (London: Methuen, 1955).
Pericles, The Arden Shakespeare, ed. F. D. Hoeniger (London: Methuen, 1969).
The Tempest, The Arden Shakespeare, ed. Frank Kermode (London: Methuen, 1954).
The Winter's Tale, The Arden Shakespeare, ed. J. H. P. Pafford (London: Routledge, 1963).

Criticism

Barton, Anne, *Essays, Mainly Shakespearean* (Cambridge: Cambridge University Press, 1994).
Bergeron, David M., *Shakespeare's Romances and the Royal Family* (Lawrence, Kansas: University Press, 1985).
Felperin, Howard, *Shakespearean Romance* (Princeton, New Jersey: Princeton University Press, 1972).
Frost, David L., 'Mouldy Tales: The Context of Shakespeare's *Cymbeline*', *Essays and Studies*, vol. 39, 1986.
Frye, Northrop, *A Natural Perspective* (New York and London: Columbia University Press, 1965).

Kahn, Coppelia, 'The Providential Tempest and the Shakesperean Family', in *Representing Shakespeare: New Psychoanalytical Essays*, ed. M. M. Schwartz and Coppelia Kahn (Baltimore: Johns Hopkins University Press, 1980).

Kermode, Frank, *Shakespeare: The Final Plays* (London: Longman Group, 1973).

Knight, G. Wilson, *The Crown of Life* (London: Methuen, 1947).

Leech, Clifford, 'The Structure of the Last Plays', *Shakespeare Survey*, vol. 11, 1958.

Mowat, Barbera A., *The Dramaturgy of Shakespeare's Romances* (Athens, Georgia: University of Georgia Press, 1976).

Nevo, Ruth, *Shakespeare's Other Language* (London: Methuen, 1987).

Palfrey, Simon, *Late Shakespeare: A New World of Words* (Oxford: Clarendon Press, 1997).

Palmer, D. J. (ed.), *Shakespeare: The Tempest*, New Casebook Series (London: Macmillan – now Palgrave, 1991).

Peterson, Douglas, *Time, Tide and Tempest: A Study of Shakespeare's Romances* (San Marino: Huntingdon Library Press, 1973).

Platt, Peter, *Reason Undiminished: Shakespeare and the Marvelous* (Lincoln, Nebraska, and London: University of Nebraska Press, 1997).

Smith, Hallet, *Shakespeare's Romances: A Study of Some Ways of the Imagination* (San Marino: Huntingdon Library Press, 1972).

Tillyard, E. M. W., *Shakespeare's Last Plays* (London: Athlone Press, 1938).

Warren, R., *Staging Shakespeare's Late Plays* (Oxford: Clarendon Press, 1990).

Index